VISUAL PUNS IN DESIGN

VISUAL PUNS IN DESIGN

**The Pun Used as a Communications Tool
by Eli Kince**

WATSON-GUPTILL PUBLICATIONS/NEW YORK

Frontispiece: Giuseppe Arcimboldo,
The Nymph Flora, ca. 1591.

First published 1982 in New York by Watson-Guptill Publications,
a division of Billboard Publications, Inc.,
1515 Broadway, New York, N.Y. 10036

Library of Congress Cataloging in Publication Data
Kince, Eli, 1953-
    Visual puns in design.
    Bibliography: p.
    Includes index.
    1. Graphic arts—History—20th century. 2. Communica-
tion in design. 3. Signs and symbols in art. 4. Puns
and punning. 5. Visual perception. I. Title.
NC998.4.K56 1982   741.6   82-16065
ISBN 0-8230-7490-0

Manufactured in U.S.A.

First Printing, 1982
1 2 3 4 5 6 7 8 9/89 88 87 86 85 84 83 82

Edited by Susan Davis
Designed by Eli Kince and Bob Fillie
Graphic production by Lesley Poliner
Set in 11 point Century Schoolbook

For my brother Edward Lee
and my daughter Sherida Elvinese

ACKNOWLEDGMENTS Books are created through the efforts of many people. Family and friends provide encouragement, peers offer criticism, and teachers give a sense of history and guidance toward the future. Each is invaluable for support. There were many others, such as the contributors and editors, who gave extra of themselves and their time.

Although it is not possible to list everyone who helped me in one way or another, I do wish to acknowledge the following people who have made outstanding contributions to me, my career, and this book: My family, who taught me to accept the challenge of life, and Bruce Ellis, Gilbert Young, John Pittman, Roger, Debbie, and Pearlene Jackson, Morris Pipkins, Rodean Frazier, Joyce Abate, Claude Debbs, Roger Van Den Bergh, Keri Keatin, Loretta Campbell, Carol Robinson, Archie Gimbell, as well as the Gresham and the Gross families, for their support during the past years. Hal Workman, my high school communications instructor who shared his wisdom with me. Gordon Salchow, the instructor and administrator who had the capacity to understand every student and the ability to consistently offer meaningful criticism and guidance. Gordon, you will always be a source of inspiration for me.

I owe a great debt to Alvin Eisenman and Andrew Forge, who patiently shared and salved my frustrations as the idea for doing my thesis on visual puns was conceived and matured into a final manuscript. To James Craig and Sharon Lee Ryder, for believing the thesis and I were both publishable. And Bradbury Thompson, who gratuitously offered his time, energy, and experience to the materialization of this project.

I also wish to acknowledge the good advice and encouragement I received from the following people who read through the manuscript: Inge Druckrey, Laura Geringer, Chris Pullman, and Georgette Ballance. Each of your thorough reviews supplied me with invaluable information. I thank Colin Forbes, Milton Glaser, Paul Rand, Lance Wyman, George Tscherny, Jim Craig, and Glenda Wharton for also reviewing the text and providing me with helpful feedback. Raymond Savignac, for producing a painting especially for the cover, and Walter Herdeg for giving this project special interest. And Vct-Graphics for performing a super-human task on the artwork.

At Watson-Guptill, I would like to thank the entire staff for doing all they could to help me complete this project. Special thanks go to Steve Kliment, David Lewis, Carole Forman, Bob Fillie, Robin Goode, and Carolyn Quinn. Above all, I would like to thank my editor, Susan Davis, without whom this book would never have been published.

CONTENTS

Bradbury Thompson, *Vitruvius II*, screen
print with red and blue interfused,
1950-1977.

FOREWORD The "pun" according to the dictionary that still bears the name of Daniel Webster, Dartmouth College, A.B. 1801, is "The humorous use of a word, or of words which are formed or sounded alike but have different meanings, in such a way as to play on two or more of the possible applications; a play on words."

Visual puns, according to this interesting and informative new book by Eli Kince, Yale University, M.F.A. 1980, are not much different than verbal puns. The same definition applies if we drop "words" and replace them with "symbols." After all, words are symbols.

Eli Kince's given name is not inappropriately the same as Eli Yale's, by coincidence. However, he received his A.B. degree from the University of Cincinnati in 1978, and he enjoyed the creation of visual puns before undergraduate college, at Glenville High School in Cleveland, Ohio, where he worked long hours on school publications and posters.

Probably Eli Kince didn't know he was actually creating something called "visual puns" until he came to the Yale graphic program, or perhaps he learned it from his mentor, Gordon Salchow, in the excellent graphics program at Cincinnati. A dedicated young designer does these things intuitively, for the sheer joy of doing them. When he attends graduate school, he is certain to learn the *names* of such things that he has been enjoying and doing well for a lifetime.

And teachers, too, discover these names at such design centers. One such visiting professor was highly pleased several years ago to learn that the structures he had been using instinctively for decades in publication design are formally called "grid systems." And to his delight, after working on a Bible for 10 years, arranging the 1,800 pages of text into phrases to be read more easily, he learned one day at Oxford University Press from the manuscript of a Princeton scholar that he had been doing something, that since classical Greek times, has been known as "colometry." This scholarly word, incidentally, does not appear in *Webster's Dictionary*.

Eli Kince was a talented student and good friend at Yale, where he produced a commendable thesis on visual puns, with support from Andrew Forge, Alvin Eisenman, Paul Rand, Inge Druckery, myself, kind librarians, and sympathetic fellow students.

In the months following graduation, he showed his thesis to James Craig, Watson-Guptill's innovative design director, who responded with enthusiasm to the idea and, equally important, with professional backing.

Late in 1981, Eli Kince discussed with me his opportunity, apprehension, and determination to develop his thesis into a book. Upon observing his plans and reviewing his own visual puns, I fully realized how much he and I had in common about this approach to graphics that now has a name and for which he planned to make a landmark explanation.

His project has required much work, much worry, and many long hours. However, with the aid of a sympathetic publisher and Susan Davis, an understanding editor, *his* conception, *his* research, *his* design, and *his* writing have now become *his* book.

And it was not only the advantage of having studied at fine universities, but also of having worked with high school publications and hometown printers, as well as having family support, that gave him the confidence to complete a work of this originality and complexity.

Eli Kince's book now provides an important illustrated definition of an effective device with which you may be inspired or amused. And with which you may work or play, but only successfully in the spirit of the latter.

Bradbury Thompson

1
PUNS
IN
PERSPECTIVE

Today's society is being bombarded with visual and verbal messages in quantities unimaginable a hundred years ago. Visual and verbal puns are becoming an increasingly important technique of modern communication. It is as if Charles Lamb's remark that puns are "a pistol let off at the ear; not a feather to tickle the intellect" is a prophecy coming true. Puns identify, inform, and sell products and ideas in a highly charged atmosphere of intense competition; they are noticed when and where audiences have become immune to many other advertising techniques.

Puns, with economical means, touch on different levels or areas of meaning at the same time in often quite unexpected ways. The resulting new connection pushes beyond conventional patterns of thought to produce surprise or delight, or both. Perhaps this explains why an increasing number of twentieth-century writers, artists, and designers like puns—because they offer ways to create precise, efficient concepts intelligently, with imagination and wit.

What Is a Pun?

The *Oxford English Dictionary* notes that the word *pun* is probably one of the clipped words, such as *mob, snob,* and *nob,* that came into fashionable slang in England in the sixteenth century or in the seventeenth century after the Restoration. *Pun* may have originated as an abbreviation of the Italian word *puntiglio,* which means "a fine point" or "quibble." But the exact origin of the word remains obscure.

The pun is not an exclusively English-language phenomenon. Puns exist in many languages. In French, *pun* is expressed by the word *calembour* or the phrase *jeu de mots* for "play on words." The Chinese and German languages also contain puns. In German, the term for *pun* is *Wortspiel,* which also means "word play." These translations are very apt because a pun is, of course, a play on words.

Puns are usually thought of as humorous word play, but they can also be serious, satiric, or ironic. A pun is made when one word is used to suggest two or more meanings or applications or when a word is used in place of a similar-appearing or similar-sounding word of a different meaning. The play, or point, is produced by sound, letter, or word manipulation.

Visual puns are not much different. The same definition applies. By substituting *symbol* for *word* (after all, words are symbols, too), we arrive at a contemporary definition that can be applied to both verbal and visual puns: (1) the use of a symbol in such a way as to suggest two or more meanings or different associations or (2) the use of two or more symbols of the same or nearly the same appearance or sound with different meanings. The pun is created when these symbols are used in a context in such a way that both meanings are possible and give added meaning to the overall statement. For a further explanation of how puns work, see Chapter 2.

Giuseppe Arcimboldo combines various forms of sea life to create this allegorical composite portrait entitled *Wasser* (water). He also painted similar portraits of land and air.

The Origins of Verbal and Visual Puns

Although the earliest records of human communication are on cave walls, the purpose of the charcoal bison and reindeer is still unknown. The drawings could have been part of a religious ceremony or mere portraits. Although we cannot know the artists' original intentions, we must assume that visual communication began when the inhabitants of the caves wanted to tell stories with these images: for example, to describe a hunting party in the field. Of course, cave and rock art is not writing. Thousands of years separated such art from the development of writing.

Writing began when a representational picture was conventionally used to stand for a word in a language. The picture of a bee, for example, was used to stand for the word *bee*. But no language can be fully accommodated by such a limited system. The breakthrough in writing occurred when a picture or mark was used to stand, not for the thing it pictured, but for a different word with the same sound. The picture of the bee, for example, was used to stand for the word *be*. *Phoneticization*, or the *rebus principle*, had been discovered, and the world had its first visual pun. The rebus principle enabled the developers of early writing systems to make another improvement—they began to phoneticize syllables. Thus, syllabic writing systems arose.

Egyptian hieroglyphics, that highly pictorial script of the Nile monuments—and the first extinct language to be fully deciphered—was both pictorial and phonetic. Both the word signs and the phonetic signs were used to record the many homonyms, word spelled and sounded alike but with different meanings—the raw material of puns, if you will—that the language contained. Thus the word for *hear* sounded the same as the one for *paint the eyes*. So, in Egyptian writing, instead of a picture of an ear being read as *ear* or *hear*, it was sometimes read as *paint the eyes*. In like manner, the sign the Egyptians used for *lute* could be used, too, to mean *good* because both were made up of the same consonants or syllables. Other word signs that were interchangeable were those for *dung beetle* and *to become*, for *flute* and *true*, for *eye* and *to make*, for *house* and *to come out*, and many more. The opportunities for multiple readings of the same word were so common that the Egyptians eventually developed another device, an unpronounced classifier, called a *determinative*, to help keep clear which reading was meant. With a language so fertile in opportunities to pun, it is not surprising to find that punning is regularly found in the literature of ancient Egypt.

Many ancient Chinese letterforms were also used to make puns in a similar manner. Their letterforms were created from patterns in nature and used images that sounded like other images when spoken.

Herd of cattle in cave painting from Jabbaren, Tassili, Central Sahara. Pastoralist period, 4500 B.C.

When early Egyptians had to express a difficult idea in pictures, they developed the rebus principle to "spell" the desired word. Because so many hieroglyphic words could be read as homonyms, Egyptian scribes made liberal use of determinative symbols to be sure their readers grasped the correct meaning. By this system the Egyptians could use the same grouping of symbols to indicate as many as ten completely different words. In the above illustration are the words for *liquid measure, rejoicing,* and *neighbors*.

From Aristotle's Paragrams to Aquinas's Spiritual Images

Although many cultures used the rebus principle to create puns for thousands of years, the Greeks can be credited with the beginning of its modern development. The first application was when they used puns on their vases and other artifacts to represent subject matter. With this practice, the role of the pun was extended from pragmatic usage as letterforms to personal and conceptual expressions. For instance, Greek vases contained puns based on mythical or allegorical subjects. The pun was no longer seen only as a representation of a word or sound, but as a viable method of presenting information.

The second important transition in the pun's development came when the Greeks began to incorporate puns into their speech and thought patterns. The Greeks were imaginative and inventive, the perfect intellectual soil in which to nurture puns, and the verbal pun began to appear in their word games and analytical treatises. Aristotle, who wrote works on logic, philosophy, natural science, ethics, politics, and poetics, discussed two or three types of puns in the eleventh chapter of his book on rhetoric. It is interesting to note that his name for them was *paragrams*, or a kind of play upon words, consisting of an alteration of one letter or group of letters in a word. One type (for example, "O steel in heart as thou are steel in name") is also discussed in Chapter 23 of Book II.

The Romans helped keep puns alive as the ancient Greek culture declined. For example, puns are discussed and analyzed in all the classical treatises of rhetoric by Cicero and by the anonymous author of *Rhetorical ad Herennium.*

The Greeks' cultural richness can be attributed in part to the fact that they worshiped a multitude of gods and goddesses. But after the assimilation of Christianity into Greco-Roman civilization, the concept of one God began to dominate, and Christianity became the primary subject matter of almost every form of visual communication. The majority of painting and sculpture that have come down to us were based on the scriptures, scribes, and saints for well over ten centuries.

Visual punning was practically ignored during the early medieval period, as pictorial illustrations of religious subject matter in Early Christian and Byzantine art did not include many puns. For instance, the fish in Early Christian art is used as a symbol of Christ. The fish was two things—a fish and Christ—but it only represented one—Christ. The fish was a symbol for Christ because the letters of the Greek word for *fish* were the initial letters of the phrase: "Jesus Christ, son of God, the Savior." Not a pun, but certainly word play and possibly word magic. The effect is similar to punning, but this sort of imagery was more used as symbols to represent one thing, rather than as puns. The fish was not meant to be two things at once, but only to symbolize Christ. Sometimes definite things, such as a serpent or a cross, opened the door to many interpretations. But deliberate visual puns were avoided as images were selected to represent

Drawn from Proto-Attic amphora, *Perseus and the Gorgons, the Murder of Nessos,* 700-600 B.C. After artists in Athens started to reproduce the human figure for ritualistic and funerary purposes, it became inevitable that it would be used on vases. In the eighth century B.C., the age of the epic and the mythical story, vases were created with stories about heroes, scenes of combat, or ceremonies in honor of gods and of departed heroes.

specific meanings or messages. For instance, a painting of a beautiful woman and child was always interpreted as the Virgin and the Christ Child.

The verbal pun had often been used since its inception for humorous purposes, and even though vernacular literature was not recorded for many centuries, merry speeches and witty tales were passed on by a strong oral tradition. Many types of word play and puns were experimented with and later included in such works as *Song of Roland, Tristan and Isolt, The Cid, The Canterbury Tales, The Decameron*, as well as many others.

The acceptance of riddles and metaphors in the scriptures by the Church and its members indirectly contributed to the acceptance of verbal puns. In fact, the Catholic Church was established on a pun: "Thou art Peter, and upon this rock I will build my church" (Matthew 16:18). *Peter*, of course, means "rock."

The verbal pun found sanction in mid-medieval literature because it allowed the manipulation of multiple meanings, an effect the religious scholars liked. To them, punning was honorable; in fact the medieval *puntiglio* was looked upon as a beauty mark, rather than a blemish. For example, a *puntiglio* was created when a word was used twice with a shift in meaning: "A young man should learn a craft, so that when he becomes an old man he need not resort to craft."

The multiple meaning created by puns was not regarded by later medieval priests and writers as primarily a vehicle for humor. They felt the effect was similar to the seriousness of the metaphors in the scriptures. In his evaluation of the teachings of Christ, the brilliant 13th-century Italian theologian St. Thomas Aquinas offered some insight into different levels of meanings in the scriptures. In his treatise, *Questiones Quodlibetales*, he states, "Any truth can be manifested in two ways: by things or by words. . . . the Scriptures contain a twofold truth. One lies in the things meant by the words used—that is the literal sense. The other in the way things become figures of other things, and in this consists the spiritual sense." The fact that double meanings of religious symbols were accepted by those who studied the scriptures made it possible for the verbal pun to adorn sermons, and it was delivered with great gravity from the pulpit as a means of emphasis and an instrument of persuasion.

Pictorial art in this period followed similar principles of using symbolic meanings for communicating messages; the viewer had to interpret the pictures or images in the paintings. Metaphors were created as various objects represented in certain religious paintings, according to E. H. Gombrich in *Symbolic Images*, were used to support or elaborate the meaning of the scriptures. For instance, he believed that the light falling through the church window in Jan Van Eych's painting, *The "Friedsam" Annunciation*, is a metaphor for the Immaculate Conception and the two styles of building stand for the Old and New Testaments. Gombrich also ex-

plained why the pictorial representation of religious subject matter did not produce the same effect as a pun: "Here as always the symbol functions as a metaphor which only acquires its specific meaning in a given context. The picture had not several meanings but one."

The Effect of the Renaissance on Visual Communication

With the birth of the Italian Renaissance, many medieval attitudes died. The following age was still a devout one, but people did not subordinate everything in this life to the life to come. The significance of the Renaissance was the pursuit of learning in languages, literature, history, and philosophy for its own end in a secular rather than a religious framework. The eventual breakaway from strictly devotional subjects brought to human communication a freedom in expression and offered such numerous ways to record images that the Greeks would have been delighted. Artists and writers began to put on canvas and in print their love for antiquity and the humanities. They wanted to recapture the classical forms, their truths and myths, and ancient Greece was their model.

The emergence of graphic art in Europe during the fifteenth century also helped free artists from the tradition of religious painting. The development of printed pictures and books was introduced in Europe five centuries after movable type was developed in China, and it slowly changed the nature of visual communication. With the creation of more imaginative work and techniques of application, visual material found a permanent home, and the printed page eventually gave birth to graphic design.

Excitement was also developing in the content of painting, which could be divided into three distinct groups: mystical and religious subjects, mythical and allegorical themes based on classical Greece, and genre scenes depicting unidentified people in local settings. There were even a number of paintings in which the content could not be explained. Patrons either invented subjects to be painted or, more often, enlisted the aid of some learned person to supply the artist with subject matter. Religious symbolism and mythical, paradoxical, and esoteric illusions portrayed the Renaissance wit as artists painted their noble content with noble forms.

It is impossible to tell how many, if any, visual puns were created during this period without actual documentation of the artists or patrons. In *Symbolic Images*, E. H. Gombrich states that he did not believe that any puns were created in Renaissance paintings. Some artists did manage to create a new way of seeing in their paintings and displayed a highly personalized style of visual communication, but not with the intent of creating visual puns. For instance, in the late fifteenth century, Hieronymus Bosch filled his pictures with grotesque and demonic figures, many representing Hell and its tortures. In the sixteenth century, El Greco broke away from the norm and painted many works in an increasingly distorted and emotional style. Later, in the eighteenth century, Francisco Goya used powerful imagery to record a highly personal view of genre scenes.

Arcimboldo, the Master of the Sixteenth-Century Visual Pun

More than two hundred years before the birth of Goya and less than twenty before that of El Greco, Giuseppe Arcimboldo was born in 1527. Like a scream unheard, Arcimboldo momentarily freed visual puns from their long captivity in devotional and mythical renderings. He took visual imagery beyond myth, allegory, and metaphor to a new world of symbolic manipulation. He brought to visual communication what Shakespeare brought to literature—timeless puns.

His consistency in both high quality and imaginative concepts convincingly shows that Arcimboldo understood not only the meaning of symbols, but also how to use them effectively. Furthermore there is no doubt, even without documentation, that some of his works were deliberate visual puns. In addition to creating puns, he single-mindedly painted apt and witty combinations of animals, fish, fruit, vegetables, among a variety of subjects that were meticulously painted and fitted together into head-and-shoulders figures that sometimes have the look of portraits. All components, whether object or creature, were grouped together to create a new world of their own. Arcimboldo also devised compositions that can be hung upside down, as well as right side up.

Giuseppe Arcimboldo, like many of his contemporaries, was influenced by the work of Leonardo da Vinci. Arcimboldo must have seen da Vinci's work earlier than most artists because there was personal and professional contact between Arcimboldo's father and the Luini family of artists. (Bernardino Luini was given a notebook of sketches by da Vinci that Arcimboldo must have seen.) In his *Storia dell'arte Italiana*, Adolfo Venturi notes that "of the great Leonardo's students, none could match this later disciple's ability to grasp and render the motion of the molecules, the internal structures of animal form. Indeed, the hand of Leonardo seems to have guided that of Arcimboldo."

The influence of da Vinci's monsters with caricatured features stayed with Arcimboldo for years. However, it wasn't until he was arranging the Wunderkammern, the collection of artifacts of Maximilian II and Rudolf II, that he developed his composite style of painting. He could have seen Indian miniatures showing animals, usually elephants, horses, and antelopes, that overlap with other animals or with human figures. Or possibly he studied the ancient Roman and Greek decorated vases and mosaics that used the same principle, which were in the archeological museum at Naples. There were even fifteenth-century illuminated manuscripts that had whimsical composites of people, animals, and plants in the form of letters. Arcimboldo may have borrowed any one of these strategies for his paintings.

Arcimboldo's *Portrait of Rudolf II as Vertumnus* (shown in color on page 97) is created in both jest and homage to his patron. Portrayed entirely in fruits and vegetables, the image suggests two things at once. Arcimboldo used images to create an effect quite different from the symbolism of his contemporaries and others centuries before and after him. In

fact, the art form closest to that of Arcimboldo that materialized before the twentieth century was created by the caricature artist Honoré Daumier, a biting political cartoonist who contributed satirical drawings to various Paris weeklies most of his life. King Philip, drawn to look like a pear, is one of Daumier's more famous caricatures (the French word for *pear* also means "fathead").

The visual pun, *The Nymph Flora*, displays Arcimboldo's imagination and wit. Completed about 1591, it stimulated great interest among his contemporaries. This attention is well documented. E. H. Gombrich must have overlooked the works of this artist and the documentation of his peers when he stated that there were no deliberate visual images created in the sixteenth century with "two divergent meanings." Comanini, one of Arcimboldo's contemporaries, questions the existence of two distinct things created by one image in his response, *Il Figino*, to *The Nymph Flora*:

> Am I Flora, or am I flowers?
> If like flowers, how then can Flora
> Have a smiling face? And if I be Flora,
> How can Flora be only flowers?
> Ah! I am not flowers, nor am I Flora,
> Yet Flora am I, and flowers.
> A thousand flowers, a single Flora,
> Living flowers, a living Flora.
> But if flowers make Flora, and Flora flowers,
> Do you know how? The flowers into Flora
> The wise painter changed, and Flora into flowers.

The word *flora* is the name of a flower goddess and also means "the plant life of a area." The painting is truly a visual pun, as well as a play on the word *flora*.

Arcimboldo's work may have been overlooked by Gombrich, as well as other art historians, because there is no distinctive style with which to compare it. His paintings do not fit comfortably in either Mannerism or the Baroque. They were not created to tell a story or recount dreams, as the former style implies. And the shock value of Arcimboldo's paintings is all that is applicable of the Baroque. His work was not presurrealistic, nor can it be attached to any of the associations typical of surrealism.

Arcimboldo's work may also have been ignored because his contemporaries considered him a "joke" and a "nonconformist." But nonconformity made Rembrandt, Vermeer, Poussin, Goya, and many others great. Why not Arcimboldo? It appears that art historians often need to compare people and artwork with something, and to compare one who is before his time with his contemporaries is inconceivable. So Arcimboldo has been virtually unknown since his death in 1593 until the second half of the twentieth century, when artists were willing and able to break away from society's constraints and when visual and verbal puns have been generally accepted and sometimes even admired.

With *The Nymph Flora*, Arcimboldo perfected his composite portrait style and also the art of punning. These possible meanings are created by this one image: *Flora* may mean a woman, the flower goddess, the plant life of a specific region and all are applicable.

From Shakespeare's Puns to Stein's Word Play

Unlike the visual pun, the verbal pun found an intellectual climate in Europe during the Renaissance that allowed it to flourish. The son of a shop owner in Stratford-upon-Avon was becoming well known as a literary and dramatic craftsman. By 1598, less than five years after the death of Arcimboldo, William Shakespeare was frequently using verbal puns in his poems, sonnets, and plays. Before he died, he created over 1,000 in his works and shaped the way we use them today.

In *Shakespeare's Pronunciation*, Helge Kökeritz identified two of Shakespeare's favorite techniques as the semantic pun and the homonymic pun. *Semantic puns* are created when one word is used in such a way that it implies two or more meanings. One way to do that is by altering the sense of a word. For example, in Shakespeare's *Cymbeline*, the two meanings of the word *rank* created a pun:

> *Cloteon*: Would he had been one of my rank!
> *Second Lord:* [*aside*] To have smelled like a fool!

In *homonymic puns* two or more words whose sounds are nearly identical but unrelated in meaning are used to create a desired effect. One of many examples in Shakespeare is found in *The Second Part of Henry the Fourth*:

> *Lord Chief Justice:* Your means are very slender,
> and your waste is great.
> *Falstaff:* I would it were otherwise; I would my means
> were greater, and my waist slenderer.

Shakespeare used puns in comic and tragic situations and also to help illustrate the complexity of thought processes in moments of tension and confusion. For instance, one of the key points of *Romeo and Juliet* is when Juliet is uncertain of the news that Romeo is dead. Shakespeare communicates her anxiety with a pun:

> Hath Romeo slain himself? Say thou but ay,
> And that bare vowel "I" shall poison more
> Than the death-darting eye of cockatrice,
> I am not I, if there be such as ay;
> Or those eyes shut, that makes thee answer ay.
> If he be slain, say ay; or if not, no.
> Brief sounds determine of my weal or woe.

Shakespeare also used puns to expose the imaginative minds and fast wit of his subjects. *The Taming of the Shrew* contains many explosive scenes in which there are battles of mind and will, and puns are used as weapons. For examples, when Petruchio first met Katharina, they argued, their tempers rose, and Katharina struck him:

Petruchio: I swear I'll cuff you, if you strike again.

Katharina: So may you lose your arms:
　　　　　If you strike me, you are no gentleman;
　　　　　And if no gentleman, why, then no arms.

Petruchio: A herald, Kate? O, put me in thy books!

Katharina: What is your crest? a coxcomb?

Petruchio: A combless cock, so Kate will be my hen.

Katharina: No cock of mine; you crow too like a craven.

The Taming of the Shrew contains a tremendous number and variety of puns and word play, from subtle innuendos to strikingly ribald statements.

However, after this heyday, word games and excessive ingenuity brought the pun into disrepute by the end of the seventeenth century, and by Joseph Addison's time in the early eighteenth century, its use was judged a fault. The English essayist, poet, and statesman expressed his disdain in *Spectator No. 16*: "The seeds of Punning are in the minds of all [men]; and though they may be subdued by reason, reflection, and good sense, they will be very apt to shoot up in the greatest genius that is not broken and cultivated by the rules of the art." Later in the same work Addison even accused the pun of being a false wit. He also believed that because the pun ". . . has sunk in one age and rose in another, it will again recover itself in some distant period of time, as pedantry and ignorance shall prevail upon wit and sense."

The verbal pun has never regained full respectability from this low esteem in the early eighteenth century. Word play did not establish a major following in nineteenth-century Victorian England, caught between the beginning of the Industrial Revolution and a conservative ruler. However, word play was being accepted in America, although without much enthusiasm. This uncertainty prompted Edgar Allen Poe to note, "Of puns it has been said that most dislike, who are least able to utter them." It wasn't until Gertrude Stein's abstractionism and construction of a language based on sound (music) and not sense helped word play become more tolerated as a serious form of literary expression.

Born in 1874, Gertrude Stein outlived Guillaume Apollinaire, who used visual play to enhance his poetry—in "It's Raining," the letters are set vertically to suggest rain—and whose art criticism influenced the Futurist and Dada art movements. Stein was a patron of prominent artists of at least seven art movements and also witnessed the two world wars. The vitality of her times stimulated her to try to reflect movement and time in words. She employed a repetitious technique based on the idea of cinematographic frames: each word changes ever so slightly, giving the illusion of continuity.

IL PLEUT

Il pleut des voix de femmes comme si elles étaient mortes même dans le souvenir

c'est vous aussi qu'il pleut merveilleuses rencontres de ma vie ô gouttelettes

et ces nuages cabrés se prennent à hennir tout un univers de villes auriculaires

écoute s'il pleut tandis que le regret et le dédain pleurent une ancienne musique

écoute tomber les liens qui te retiennent en haut et en bas

Apollinaire's poem, *It's Raining*, plays on the subject with its letters arranged to suggest rain.

Although Gertrude Stein was very prolific, much of her work was not published until after her death in 1946, and the word/sound games she created did not really begin to catch the ears of a following until the second half of the century. By that time word play had established a strong hold in literature and speech, and verbal puns were ready to be united with images in a new application of creative art in advertising.

The Explosion of Visual Play in the Twentieth Century

With the profound explosion of art in the twentieth century, the visual pun began to appear more frequently in painting, sculpture, and architecture. The Industrial Revolution created the social and economic changes that motivated artists to rethink the function of their work in a world in which changes and new discoveries were the only constant things. Artists sought to define their part in that evolving world. It seemed that civilization was abandoning humanity for technology, and artists throughout the Western world began to seek ways to fuse the sensitivity of art with the analytical approach of science. Artists also wanted to reflect the new products and new means of human communication in their work. Artists were no longer slave stone carvers, religious renderers, or pets of patrons, but rebellious thinkers who set their own courses in defining the role and function of art in a new age.

In 1905, Henri Matisse led a group of painters to exhibit in the Salon d'Automhe in Paris. The paintings were simple in design yet so brilliant in color that a critic described the artists as *fauves*, or "wild beasts." And so a new art movement began. The Fauves were stimulated by the newly appreciated woodcarvings, sculptures, and textiles from Africa, Polynesia, and Central and South America. The unexpected shapes and colors from these non-European cultures suggested new ways of communicating emotion and helped lead artists out of the Renaissance and into a new age of experimentation.

Various pockets of artists began to explore new ways of visual representation. The expressionist Max Beckmann rendered distorted and simplified figures to stimulate reactions of terror and pity. In Cubist painting, Pablo Picasso, Georges Braque, and Juan Gris were concerned with building form, and Vasily Kandinsky sought to use forms that relied on total nonobjectivity in his abstract paintings.

The advent of the First World War influenced the ideology of the Italian school of Futurism. The 1909 manifesto of the poet Filippo Marinetti proclaimed a new art of "violence, energy, and boldness." The Futurists had an extreme dislike of all traditional art and demanded modernism. In the words of the Futurist sculptor Umberto Boccioni, "We propose . . . to sweep from the field of art all motifs and subjects that have already been exploited . . . to destroy the cult of the past . . . to despise utterly every form of imitation . . . to extol every form of originality . . . to render and glorify the life of today, unceasingly and violently transformed by victorious science."

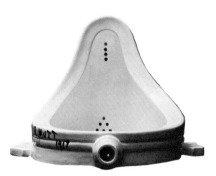

The usual utilitarian function of a urinal is given a bizarre twist by Marcel Duchamp in *Fountain*.

In *Parte II, Rue Larrey*, Marcel Duchamp cleverly positions a door that can never completely close off the room in which the viewer stands.

Marcel Duchamp's moustache on a reproduction of the *Mona Lisa*, known as *L.H.H.O.Q.*, is a witty attack on the attitudes of Renaissance artwork. He questioned the values of the public and the artist, as well as the value of art.

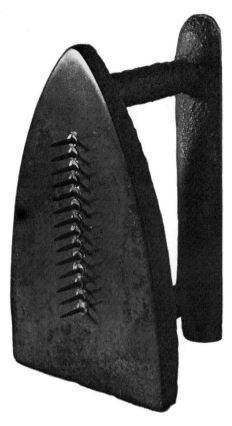

Using principles very similar to those used in the word games of Gertrude Stein and Apollinaire, the Futurist painters wanted to present movement and passage of time on canvas that reflected the active and mechanized society they lived in. The Dutch painter Piet Mondrian renounced all representational elements in painting to concentrate only on color, line, and shape. Kasimir Malevich sought to take Mondrian's concept further in a style he called "Suprematism." He wanted to stimulate pure feeling and perception without using any natural forms. The Rumanian sculptor Constantin Brancusi, working in marble, metal, and wood, carried abstraction beyond the point of representation. The First World War began in 1914, and the artists scattered, but not before the creation of at least seven new art movements since the Fauves' first exhibition. The art world had experienced an intensive revolution that set the tempo for change and experimentation for at least the next fifty years. This development of individual artistic freedom provided the foundation for personal expression and, ultimately, for visual puns.

Witticism and visual play began to take a firm hold in the art world shortly after the beginning of the First World War. In several places at nearly the same time—Zurich, Barcelona, and New York in 1916 and 1917—a number of artists independently stated their disgust with the war and with life in general by making works of non-art. This art movement was called "Dada." For example, Marcel Duchamp drew a moustache on a photograph of the *Mona Lisa* as a direct and witty attack against the ideals of the Renaissance. Dada, according to Duchamp, was "a metaphysical attitude . . . a sort of nihilism . . . a way to get out of a state of mind—to avoid being influenced by one's environment, or by the past: to get away from *clichés*—to get free."

Dada artists began to explore the spontaneity of intuitive expression. In contrast with what appeared as the reasoned, formal aim and cool objectivity of Cubism and abstract art, they expressed the whimsical, fantastic, humorous, sardonic, and absurd. Upon further exploration of the optical world of compositional analysis, these artists allowed their imaginations to run free. Personal expression and interpretation were now firmly imbedded within the consciousness of the individual artist.

Before the conclusion of the war, Marcel Duchamp used his wit, including the making of puns, to express the irony of objects and their functions. Witness the playfulness in *Parte II, Rue Larrey* and *Fountain*. Earlier in *Jokes and Their Relation to the Unconscious*, Freud's observation that "jokes have not received nearly as much philosophical consideration as they deserve in view of the part they play in our mental life" was validated, and Duchamp led the way. In a manner not much different than that of Giuseppe Arcimboldo, the artist began to create composites, not only bringing together images, but materials. Picasso invented the art of collage. Antoine Pevsner and his brother Naum Gabo brought together various pieces of modern materials in their artwork to reflect their culture; they called their work "Constructivism."

Man Ray transformed a utilitarian item into a work of art by adhering tacks to its face and sardonically calling it *Cadeau.*

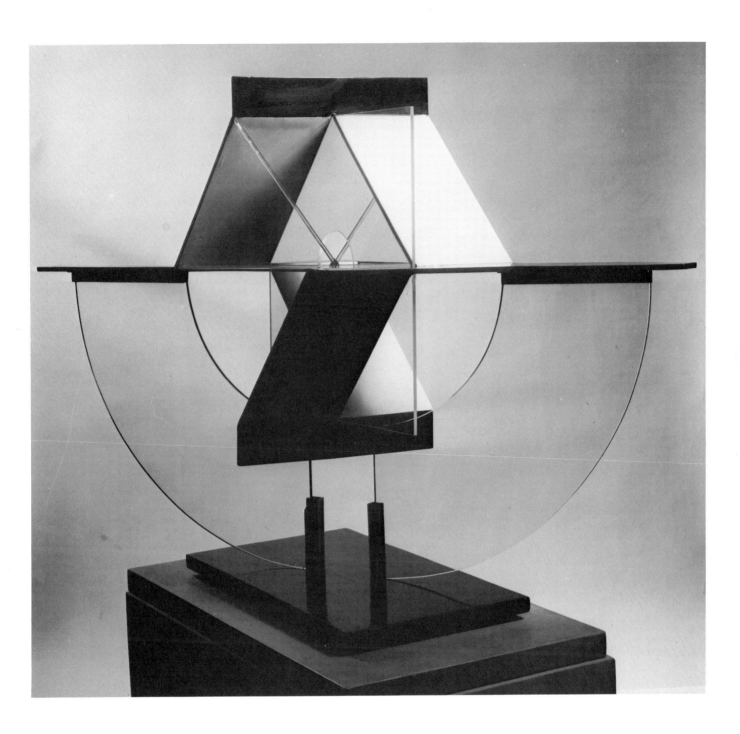

Naum Gabo explored ways of viewing
volume and space, as well as possible
uses for various modern materials in
*Construction in Space with Balance on
Two Points*.

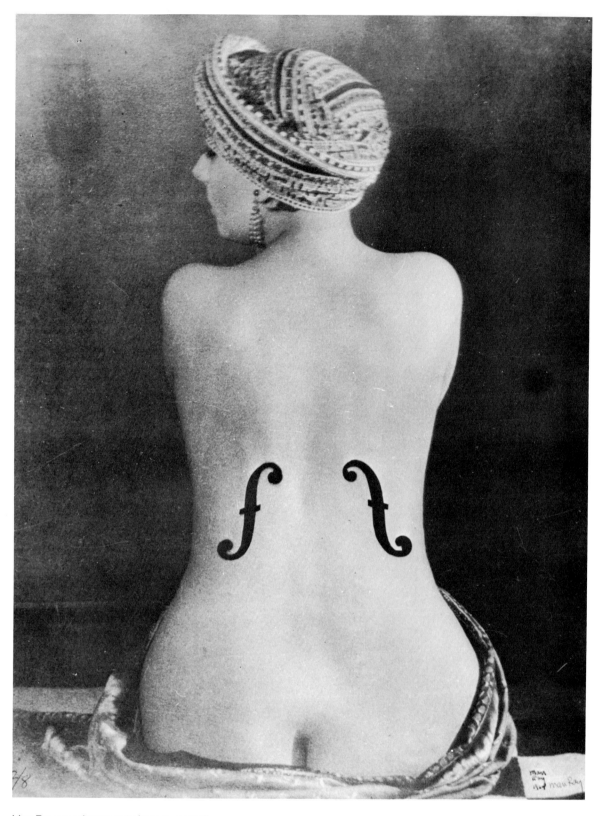

Man Ray pays homage to Ingres, as well as to women, in *Violon d'Ingres*. The pun effect is created when multiple associations are united in a single concept.

As the tension created by the First World War began to subside, artistic statements and movement became milder. The more relaxed atmosphere encouraged the general expression of playful wit and humor in artwork.

The Visual Pun Matures With the Visual Arts

Surrealism surfaced in 1924. The artists sought, according to H. W. Janson, "pure psychic automatism . . . intended to express . . . the true process of thought . . . free from the exercise of reason and from any aesthetic or moral purpose." They were not successful because it is impossible to transpose a dream from the unconscious directly to the canvas without some degree of control. But they did stimulate several novel techniques for soliciting and exploiting chance effects. Max Ernst's collages may have influenced Man Ray to create the pun *Violon d'Ingres* in 1924. Created in that same year, Constantin Brancusi's *Torso of a Young Man* is also a visual pun. However, the artist who had the most profound effect on image play and visual puns was the Belgian Surrealist painter René Magritte. As Suzi Gablik states in *Magritte:* "His life had been a solitary posture of immense effort: to overthrow our sense of the familiar, to sabotage our habits, to pull the real world on trial."

Although all of René Magritte's paintings were not visual puns, but more like visual metaphors, they did have a disconcerting effect. Whether or not they had a second meeting, they did call for a second look. Gablik further states the Magritte was a person who "liked to refuse the name of artist, saying that he was a man who *thought*, and who communicated his thought by means of painting, as others communicated it by writing music or words." Magritte wanted to make thought visible through the use of images in a way that no artist had done before. He felt that his work was unique and not applicable to any specific period or movement, calling it "facile and false" to link a certain branch of Surrealism with fantastic or fabulous art. "Bosch painted ideas which his contemporaries held about monsters. . . . Bosch was a 'religious realist,' in the way that today there are 'social realists' who 'express' the most 'up-to-date' or traditional ideas and feelings, like justice, nuclear power, industry, and so on. . . . *I don't paint ideas. I describe*, insofar as I can, by means of painted images. . . . " His painting *La Viol*, which is a visual pun, combines imagery that illustrates his philosophy of describing ideas. In a manner similar to Arcimboldo, he pulled together visual elements to describe an attitude.

In 1931, Alexander Calder brought together steel wire and aluminum in a form of art he called "mobiles." The freedom of movement unleashed by this prolific and versatile artist motivated others. Henri Matisse began making cutout shapes, and Paul Klee worked his way from lines to colors. John Hartfield blended images to create photomontages, and Pablo Picasso magically produced a bull's head out of a bicycle handle bar and seat. Later Picasso used an automobile for a baboon's head. Visual puns were being created more frequently as the new materials of a new era gave them a new beginning.

Constantine Brancusi's *Torso of a Young Man* suggests a tree trunk, in addition to its phallic image.

René Magritte also produced a risqué image in *La Viol* by substituting one set of symbols to blatantly suggest another meaning.

The Union of Visual and Verbal Puns

Until the twentieth century, visual and verbal puns had never been used together to achieve the same end beyond their primative function as pictorial inscriptions. The closest they may have come to a consistent usage was during the medieval period when stained glass windows symbolically contained metaphoric images. It wasn't until the development of the poster, a product of the Industrial Revolution, that both visual and verbal puns would begin to serve the same master.

Unlike past artworks, the poster was not intended to last, to be an isolated, unique image; it was meant to be a product of its time, to last but a moment, to be issued in many, but discardable copies. Often used as a weapon of protest, posters were hung in the streets and accepted by the public, while museums, such as the Louvre, refused to hang the paintings created by the same artists. (Toulouse-Lautrec, among others, was confronted with this problem.) The poster took art out of the confines of academe and brought it to the masses. According to the German critic and philosopher Walter Benjamin: "What the modern means of reproduction have done is destroy the authority of art and to remove it—or, rather, to remove its image which they reproduce—from any preserve. For the first time ever, images of art have become ephemeral, ubiquitous, insubstantial, available, valueless, free." But the poster had limitations. It had to be legible, and its potential for innovation was limited to the receptive capacity of the public. It wasn't until such artists as El Lissitzky, Piet Zwarf, and later Herbert Matter and Armin Hofman began to explore the visual capabilities of posters that they became an indispensable tool in a growing profession—graphic design. Many of the fine artists at the turn of the twentieth century became either part-time or full-time graphic designers, who brought to the profession an attitude of individualism, as well as an intellectual and visual curiosity that would unite visual and verbal puns. And they had new and powerful patrons in the developing corporations.

As the scope of the graphic designer's work expanded to include all forms of printed matter—brochures, catalogs, books, magazines, newspapers, advertisements, packaging, emblems, logos, exhibitions, indicators on machines, scientific illustrations, and film images—visual communicators began to use verbal and visual puns. In 1946, in *Thoughts on Design*, Paul Rand became one of the first designers to promote the visual pun: "Where a double meaning is projected graphically, [the visual pun] may be informative and entertaining as well." Rand, Bradbury Thompson, and Raymond Savignac have been creating visual puns for decades. They have combined verbal and visual imagery to make an impact, to captivate and to convince, while at the same time establishing standards of visual communication that are based on a knowledge of the history of art and insight into the future.

Fifty years after the practical development of offset printing at the beginning of the twentieth century, techniques were developed so that it be-

The likelihood of ever seeing the visual similarity of a bull's head and a bicycle seat makes this pun, *Bull's Head* by Picasso, hard to forget.

Raymond Savignac captures a stereotype about chess players as he unifies the person with the game in this illustration.

Picasso stretched his imagination to produce *Baboon and Young*, with an automobile grille for the baboon's face and snout.

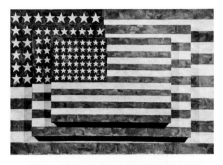

came less expensive to print images than to set type in the same space. Because of mass reproductive capabilities, pictorial images could replace type on billboards. This trend reached its peak during the mid-1950s, and in Europe, the American mass media influenced a new art movement called "Pop Art." During the social unrest in America in the following decade, Pop Art exploded. The public was saturated with all forms of printed materials, particularly advertising, photography, illustrations, and comic strips. Roy Lichtenstein exploited the last, and Jasper Johns, one of Pop's pioneers, made us look at common objects in a monumental way, such as in *Painted Bronze*. In a fashion similar to Magritte's, he made us question the difference between image and reality in *The Three Flags*.

Graphic designers also took the 1960s as a time to explore new ways to communicate, as advertisers gave them the freedom to produce less traditional visual statements. For example, Herb Lubalin created strong images with word play and graphics in his AIGA Survival Show poster of 1971. The application of flies to the word *left* reinforces the message. Tony Palladino's poster on the same subject (see page 93 top) goes a step further. His combination of image and word in a child's game of knock-knock communicates that war is no game and has no winners. Designers began to use images to challenge viewers and bring them into the argument. Bob Gill's poster to persuade people not to go to a cricket game (see page 130) had a simple type format. Yet using a pun for such a serious topic gave the message more impact and made it memorable.

In no other time in history has there been such a concentration of images or such a density of printed information. As John Berger summarized in *Ways of Seeing:* "One may remember or forget these messages, but briefly one takes them in, and for a moment they stimulate the imagination by way of either memory or expectation." We see them as "we turn the page, as we turn a corner, as a vehicle passes us. . . . But we accept the total system of publicity images as we accept an element of climate." It is more likely than not that visual puns will continue to grow in use and in popularity as the need for communicating increases. As societies become more visually literate and international symbols take effect, what could be more efficient, memorable, and universal than the visual pun that speaks in two different ways at the same time.

Not a pun, Jasper Johns' *Painted Bronze*—a Savarin coffee can with brushes—is a conscious play on the tools of the art world.

In *The Three Flags* Jasper Johns again questions the reality of ideas: Is a painted flag a flag or a painting of a flag?

A verbal pun can be enhanced by the selection of letterforms and other visual techniques, as Herb Lubalin shows in his poster for the 1971 AIGA Survival Show.

The Annual of
The American Institute
of Graphic Arts

AIGA
Graphic Design
USA: 3

Combining the "oldest form of wit" with graphic design is not an easy task. Putting intuitive reactions to puns into words can be just as difficult. To understand fully how puns work, you must first understand what puns are, how they are created, and what effects can be achieved with them. Such information is valuable because it will help you *consistently* create successful visual puns.

How Puns Work

The phenomenon that one symbol can have two or more meanings or that two or more symbols can have similar or identical images but different meanings is the *essence* of a pun. A verbal pun is created by a single phonetic form with two meanings—two strings of thought held together by an acoustic knot. Visual puns are created the same way, but instead of a phonetic form, a symbol that can be seen must offer at least two different associations that are able to enhance the message because they are appropriately applicable. Whether the multiple meanings associated with the pun are derived from the same source—such as flipping an *n* to be a *u*— or from different sources—as when pictures of doughnuts are used for the *o's* in the words "Donut Shop"—is irrelevant provided the derivations are far enough apart to be incompatible. The *pun effect* happens when the viewer becomes aware that one or more symbols have created two or more possible meanings or associations applicable in one context. The mind fluctuates between the multiple associations because they are often conflicting in meaning, yet applicable to the overall message.

Take the famous epitaph W.C. Fields wrote for himself: "On the whole, I'd rather be here than in Philadelphia." The pun is created by mentally substituting *hole* for *whole* and by understanding the different associations in W.C. Fields's attitude toward Philadelphia. The more you are aware of Fields's long-term attacks on the nature and quality of life in Philadelphia, the more effective this particular pun is. To make still another pun, it is the last word: the summation of a persistent attitude in one phrase. The pun effect is created when the mind replaces *whole* (which refers to totalness, completeness), with the word *hole* (a physical opening, in this instance, a grave). When the word *whole* is spoken in this context, two meanings are created, and they become interchangeable. It is as if they occupy the same space at the same time. The mind vacillates between the two meanings, one of which is conceptual, the other, physical. This pun demonstrates how two possible meanings can be active simultaneously, on two separate planes but in one space.

A visual pun, like a verbal pun, exists in the juxtaposition of two possibilities. The effect of a visual pun is akin to that experienced by someone observing Edgar Rubin's famous face/vase optical illusion. In Rubin's image, there is a dual reading of the figure/ground relationship, so that the image flops back and forth. At one moment the vase is the image focused on, and the space around it becomes the background; the next moment

Paul Rand combines letters and images to create a play on the letters *AIGA* for the book jacket of the American Institute of Graphic Arts third annual.

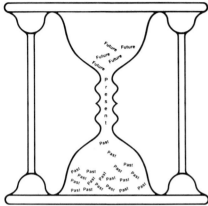

the two faces are in the foreground, and the space between them is the supporting scene.

Although images are not combined in many visual puns in such an ambiguous fashion as those in Rubin's vase, using puns offers the designer a chance to explore fresh ways of communicating a concept or way of seeing and thinking. For example, the *Hourglass* is an old story told in a new way by the combination and substitution of symbols. Taking off on Rubin's concept of two profiles that create another object, Eli Kince makes a statement about the passage of time. The two faces create an hourglass, in which words are used instead of sand to signify the movement of both sand and time.

In addition, a pun can be too efficient and lose its effectiveness. Puns frequently depend on a certain degree of surprise or shock value. Sometimes the absence of mystery leaves no surprises. Sigmund Freud suggested that the best jokes are the ones almost missed. It is the delayed reaction that increases one's enjoyment. Freud also believed that humor is created only when the "multiple use . . . might through only some difficulty be brought under the concept of double meaning."

Symbols and Communication

The visual symbol is the basic unit used to create visual puns. As letters are combined in a certain order to create words, symbols can be put together to create messages. How we respond to those symbols depends on the intellectual associations they trigger.

Symbols affect us daily; they represent all aspects of our existence, tangible and intangible—our senses and our desires, our weaknesses and our strengths. Symbols have the ability to represent something else by association, resemblance, or convention, especially when a material object is used to represent the intangible, as in the smoke from incense, which can be read as a symbol of certain religious ceremonies. Symbols can be represented in simplified or abstract forms, which offer the designer a wide range of possibilities to choose from. If any image is seen enough, it has the ability to become a symbol. However, the meaning of a symbol can change, or the symbol can stay the same, and what it represents can change. For instance, smiles have been called a symbol of our affections, but there are situations where the opposite is true. A smile can just as often conceal distrust and distaste. An example of a symbol that has remained constant is on the American flag; although the number of states and stars have changed, the thirteen stripes are still just as Betsy Ross conceived them.

Anything can be a symbol. The Quaker Oats logo is a perfect example of how a symbol can evolve from images of people. The original is indicative of a representational art form in which detail was evident. It was hoped that the attributes of a religious group, symbolized by a form of dress, would be reflected in the Quaker Oats product: honor, tradition, purity.

Edgar Rubin drew many variations on this theme of a vase created out of two faces, or vice versa. The ambiguity set up creates an effect similar to that created by a pun. In both pun and illusion, two truths can occur in the same space.

Here Eli Kince develops Rubin's vase principle into a pun. It is interesting to note that the two faces and hourglass are still legible when the image is upside down.

1877

1946

1970

For more than nine decades, the Quaker Oats logo has been able to communicate basically the same message—that of honor, purity, and tradition—although the original image has been considerably modified.

But as time passed, the logo evolved into a stylized, near-abstract symbol of a Quaker (headshot only), with hat and scarf.

You can create visual messages by translating figures, objects, and ideas into visual forms through the use of lines, shapes, and color. How you present those visual forms, alone or in combination, can influence the message to be conveyed. Observe what happens to a silhouetted wine bottle when it is combined with other images. With wine glasses, the bottle suggests romance or celebration. Present it near a steering wheel, and the implication is drastically altered.

Through careful selection, symbols that communicate more than one meaning can be used to create puns. These are called *key symbols*. To locate and use key symbols effectively, you must be aware of what you want to communicate and the symbols your targeted audience is familiar with. There are no rigid rules; your only limitation is the boundaries of your imagination. Successful designers have developed as much skill and insight in using symbols as writers have with words.*

It is not easy to form a string of words that can bring pictures to mind or to create an image that can make a person think, but it is possible to develop such a solid foundation in your understanding of symbols that you will be able to create puns comfortably. The most important consideration is the associations implicit in the images and their arrangement in the creation of symbols.

How Symbols Are Made

Visual symbols are composed of the three basic visual elements of lines, shapes, and colors, but what they can communicate is limitless.

Line. The line can communicate direction, motion, speed, texture, as well as physical and emotional traits, depending on how the line is used. If it's horizontal, it can be a horizon, while a diagonal line might suggest a hill or a challenge. Curved lines can suggest waves. A jagged line might be ferocious teeth or imply erratic behavior.

Shape. Geometric shapes—the circle, the square, and the triangle—resemble objects from nature in an abstract form. These shapes, when combined with lines, give you more options to create additional symbols. The circle, likened to the sun and the moon, has an earthy character that communicates continuity, eternity, and peace, while also suggesting motion

*A point of clarification is needed here. Visual puns may include a play on words that relies on a similarity of sound. However, verbal symbols must not be confused with the visual symbols used to record words graphically. Verbal symbols in many of Shakespeare's plays rely on the similarity in the sound of the words to create puns. But once they are translated into visual symbols (the written word), the similarity is hampered by the spelling of the words. For instance, the visual symbols of "Ay," "Eye," and "I" (used in the quotation from *Romeo and Juliet* on page 18) do not look similar enough to be called visual puns. But once they are retranslated into verbal symbols that are heard, they can work once again as puns.

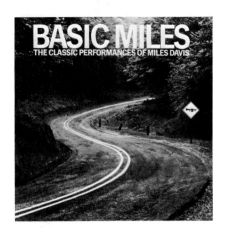

and sensuality. The square offers a completely opposite point of view. It's static and evokes a sense of stability and security. The triangle, however, can communicate a clear warning to be cautious—danger ahead—or it can take on the menacing, piercing quality of an arrow. It can also helpfully point directions.

Color. The moods associated with nature's spectrum give additional "personality" to a symbol. The sun: red for warmth, excitement. The sky: blue appears cool, and calm; it suggests loyalty. Other associations with color are related to what we've been conditioned to culturally. For instance, in Western countries, yellow implies cowardice, whereas in China it connotes wisdom.

Because every image can produce a different association or meaning, our opportunities for creating symbols by the use of lines, geometric shapes, and colors are endless. For instance, the United States highway-sign system has used color coding and uniform shapes with such consistency that the recognition of traffic directions is now almost subliminal. Red always means "stop—danger." And green "go—safety." The triangle, combined with a cautionary color, yellow, has come to denote "yield."

Maintaining the Integrity of Symbols

Visual integrity refers to the appropriateness of the symbols selected, the intent of the message, and the ability of the visual elements to work together to achieve a purpose. For instance, the variety of buildings in a large metropolis like New York City seems in character with the variety of lifestyles in the city. A building in which the facade, carpentry, and furniture reflect the style of a particular era, such as Art Deco, can have more design integrity than a building that combines various art styles. Sometimes the question of integrity is answered by a question of validity: Why take this approach?

Whenever we create puns with symbols, it is important to maintain the initial integrity of the symbols used. The concept of integrity relies on visual subjectivity: What one person may see, another may not. But in analyzing how symbols have integrity, we may look at the problem in three basic ways: (1) integrity of the whole, (2) integrity of parts, and (3) integrity of multiple usage. Within each area there are basic principles that may be applied to the ways symbols can be used to create visual puns.

Integrity of the Whole. The first way of maintaining integrity is a comparative process based on set standards or established rules. Well-designed letterforms are a perfect example. If we study a particular typeface, such as Helvetica, we find common thicknesses in all the vertical and horizontal strokes and optically corrected letter heights and counterspaces so that they appear the same, as well as similarities in the endings of certain letters. These consistencies give Helvetica letterforms a particular character or style.

CBS Records took advantage of the familiarity of highway signage to create a play between words and images on this album cover for Miles Davis.

Tony Palladino plays with the vernacular term ''cracking up'' to create this play on word and image for a book jacket, which was later adapted for the movie.

In this family Christmas card Joseph Bottoni manipulates letters to suggest sound and movement.

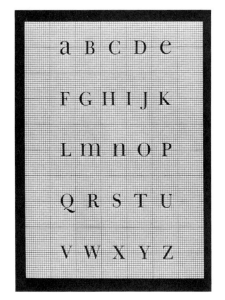

Letterforms may be considerably altered and still maintain their integrity. For instance, the capital letter A can be visually altered by lowering the crossbar, removing the crossbar, or filling in the counterspaces until it's a solid triangle. Even with these substantial changes it still can reflect the character of the remaining twenty-five letters. But the alteration must be appropriate to the context and the purpose.

Each time a symbol is altered, a new association is possible. If the altered form is effective in communicating two or more associations that are all applicable to the message, while maintaining the integrity of the selected symbols, then a successful pun is created. If the integrity is lost in the process of adding associations, then the result may be some other form of image play, but not a pun. For instance, an arrowhead can be the first letter A in the word *arrowhead* and create a pun. But a clown's cone-shaped hat used for the A in the word *hat* would not be a pun. The former brings detail and additional information to the word *arrowhead* because people see and think *arrow*, whereas in the latter the response is only *hat*. The unfamiliarity of clown's hats, plus the fact that the word *clown* is not associated with the word *hat*, leaves too many questions unanswered for a pun to take effect.

Integrity of Parts. Another way to maintain integrity is by avoiding mutilating symbols while attempting to manipulate them. There is a difference. Manipulating symbols can be achieved by shrinking, enlarging, condensing, elongating, positioning, and combining whole symbols or parts of symbols. Arcimboldo's *The Nymph Flora* (page 2) is a clear example of how this effect can be achieved. His genius is seen in the organization and placement of symbols. The floral-composite portrait in the image of a woman is actually a multiple pun. The woman's name *Flora* refers to the Roman goddess of flowers, Flora, and to the word *flora*, meaning "the plantlife of a specific region."

However, clever ideas do not always create puns, especially if a symbol has been mutilated. Simply adding or cutting away complete parts of symbols will not produce puns—even if the result is a new symbol. The only thing that happens is that a new symbol is born out of the destruction of an old one. In order to maintain the integrity of parts when creating puns, the original symbol must enhance, improve, or bring additional meaning to the overall statement or message. Or in the case of two or more symbols combined to create a new symbol, a common ground must be found that produces additional associations through their pairing. Here is an example of how the integrity of parts can be lost through mutilation. Try to create a pun with only one part of Arcimboldo's *The Nymph Flora*. Cut the contour of a woman's face out of a flower petal and call it *Flora*. The result, however, could never be a pun. It would only be a silhouette, an effect similar to a shadow.

The Integrity of Multiple Usage. The third approach to maintaining integrity is not much different from the second approach except that it

Instead of using a total of 52 letterforms, Bradbury Thompson suggests that we only use twenty-six in this poster for Westvaco. The alphabet created in ancient Rome did not contain any lower-case letters, only capitals, so that each letter had only one symbol.

Implements can be used to symbolize a profession. In this poster for a Yale art show, Eli Kince assembled artists' tools to symbolize six different disciplines.

Even the murmur of a sigh or the hush of a whisper can be interpreted by the graphic arts. Type and design on this page suggest the tantalizing, flattened-out moment of suspense when a sneeze is about to happen.

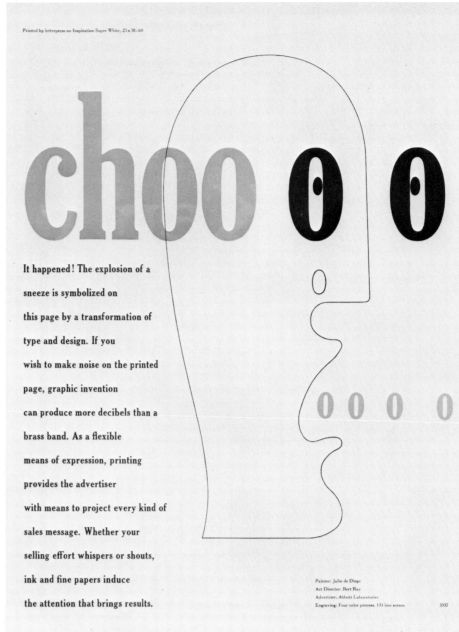

choo o o

It happened! The explosion of a sneeze is symbolized on this page by a transformation of type and design. If you wish to make noise on the printed page, graphic invention can produce more decibels than a brass band. As a flexible means of expression, printing provides the advertiser with means to project every kind of sales message. Whether your selling effort whispers or shouts, ink and fine papers induce the attention that brings results.

Painter: Julio de Diego
Art Director: Bert Ray
Advertiser: Abbott Laboratories
Engraving: Four color process, 133 line screen   3537

Bradbury Thompson captures the shattering effect of a sneeze in this illustration for Westvaco.

The National Park Service uses a pun to reinforce the international "no smoking" sign.

Using an evergreen tree on this Season's Greetings card, Clarence Lee plays on the sound similarity between *tree* and *three*.

depends on many elements to achieve a desired effect. The basic principle is that when many elements are combined, whether they are from the same or from varied sources, they must bring additional information or associations to the overall statement or message. If a castle were built out of sand, for example, all it would be is a sand castle and not a pun. Sand is not to a castle what flowers are to *The Nymph Flora*. The sand offers no additional meaning.

Now if a sand castle were built with knights' heraldic shields and weaponry, the message would then reflect the castle's purpose—to protect its inhabitants. Honor and nobility would also be suggested, adding a meaning very close to a castle's symbolic message.

How Symbols Are Used to Create Puns

How much a symbol can be tampered with depends on the initial legibility of the specific symbol and on one's familiarity with it. Unlike words, images offer a wide range for possible alteration. One image can replace another by substitution; images can be combined by overlapping, overexposing, or connecting them. And they can be manipulated by stretching or shrinking them, or by using other visual techniques.

Substituting Symbols. Substitution is effective when one symbol takes the place of another and becomes the key symbol that activates a pun effect. A word, phrase, or image can be used in place of another word, phrase, or image. The new symbols must be able to communicate at least two meanings or associations, with each adding to the overall message before it can work as a pun. For instance, many Americans are aware of the National Park Service's campaign to prevent forest fires. Smokey, a bear injured in a forest fire, became the Service's mascot and symbol of fire prevention. Recently, however, the service has adopted the international symbol for "no smoking" in their campaign as well. The headline of a recent ad read, "No ifs, ands or butts." The message is simple: no cigarettes. The message plays on the original line's connotation of "no excuses."

Other good examples of substitution are Clarence Lee's Christmas cards for 1973 and 1975. In the first one, an evergreen tree, a symbol of Christmas, is substituted for the last digit, 3. Lee plays with the similarity between the word *tree* and the numeral *3*. Visually the card communicates a clear message. In the second card a similar substitution technique has a different effect. Instead of using sound, Lee forces the viewer to make a numerical connection. The mind translates the hand to read *5*. The pun works because many people have used their fingers to count with.

Pentagram created an interesting effect on the book jacket for *George Nelson on Design*. Unlike an anagram created when a word or phrase is formed by reordering the letters of another word or phrase, Pentagram allowed two letters in one word to serve as both a word ending and a word by printing the last two letters of the longer word in a separate color. The color creates the substitution and the pun.

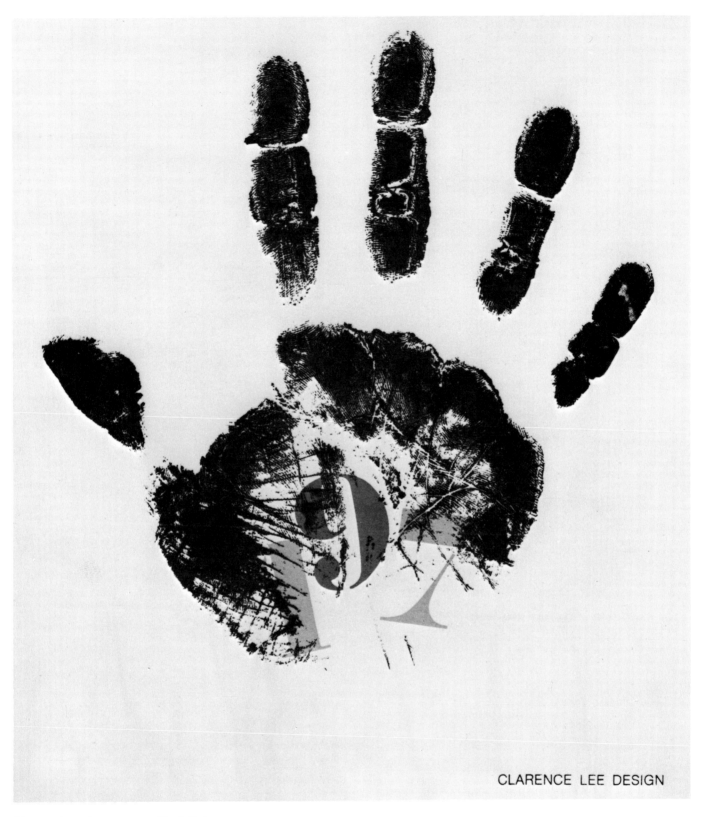

CLARENCE LEE DESIGN

Clarence Lee plays a game with digits in
this New Year's card for 1975.

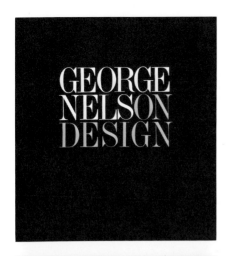

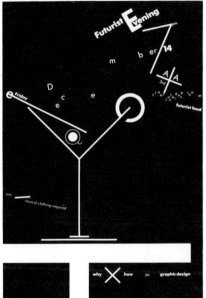

Combining Symbols. Another way to create a successful pun is to take a symbol from one source and add it to another to create a meaningful new symbol. It is not necessary that the two symbols be incompatible. The pun effect can be achieved simply by confronting quantitatively different scales of images, provided that the two original meanings differ sufficiently from one to the other to create the pun effect when compared. In Braldt Bralds's *Life Begins at 90*, the objective was to illustrate a statement about the relationship between age and mental attitude. His technique was a simple one, but the message is profound. The toddler and the beard provide qualitatively different frames of reference.

Key symbols can also be combined in such a way that they make statements about concepts and other styles of communication. For example, the Futurist artists created images of people and entire scenes with letterforms and other symbols found in a type foundry during the early part of the twentieth century. Eli Kince's *Martini Glass with Stirrer* is a pun that evokes that era. The objective was to create a poster inviting people to a Yale University cocktail party, the theme of which was a Futuristic evening. The result spells out Yale.

Manipulating Symbols. The techniques for manipulating symbols to create successful pun effects are boundless. They include enlargements, reductions, other distortions, as well as various combinations. Another interesting manipulative procedure is the animation of concepts or ideas. The Best logo designed by Chermayeff & Geismar Associates is one, and the crawl poster designed by Eli Kince is another.

The Best logo plays on the concept of growth, with the letters visually illustrating that concept. Growth is communicated by manipulating the scale of the letters. However, the logo is not a pun because the letters do nothing more than visually translate the word.

Sometimes puns can be created by the placement of images within a format. In the "crawl" poster, type is used to portray both the smoke and a person. The type was manipulated not only by the placement of the letterforms, but also by tilting the letters.

A similar pun effect was created by Peter Millward for the University of Houston's *Forum Magazine*. In the illustration for the article, "Saul Bellow and the Liberal Tradition in American Literature," Bellow's name is shown in an extremely condensed type style, to suggest both a capital L for "liberal" and an unextended bellows (see page 77).

Dividing Puns into Three Categories

There are essentially three distinct categories of puns: the *literal pun*, the *suggestive pun*, and the *comparative pun*. All types of puns belong to one of these three groups. The definitions are simple to understand and easy to apply. The best way to identify the specific types of pun is first to locate the key symbol or symbols that cause the pun effect. The next is to determine how the symbol or symbols work to create multiple meanings.

Braldt Bralds brings together youth and age to create a witty pun in this poster.

Pentagram creates an interesting effect on this book jacket by simply changing the color of two letters.

Eli Kince creates a pun in this Futurist party announcement. The letters suggest objects in much the same manner that the Futurists did in the early twentieth century.

if you're
caught
in smoke

crawl

BEST

In a poster for Yale's fire marshal, Eli Kince manipulates letterforms to suggest both smoke and people.

Chermayeff & Geismar Associates use changes in scale to create a metaphoric logo for Best, Inc.

If the multiple meanings or associations are created basically by one symbol or one effect and the multiple meanings literally repeat the message and themselves, the result is a literal pun. If one symbol is used to create multiple meanings that are slightly or greatly different from one another, the result is a suggestive pun. And if there is more than one key symbol or effect and the pun effect is created because of a visual similarity, the result is a comparative pun. An example of each follows.

The Literal Pun. When the effect that creates the pun literally upholds the primary meaning of the message, a literal pun is the result. The key symbol can create two meanings or be two things at once, but they both must repeat the initial meaning, with no loss of the original message. Milton Glaser's promotional design for New York City is a good literal pun. By substituting the romantic symbol of the heart for the word, Glaser brings to the phrase an affectionate connotation that is achieved in a most efficient manner.

The Suggestive Pun. When symbols create that almost magical feeling that you are seeing one thing with two meanings at the same time, you have witnessed a suggestive pun. There are many ways to produce them (see Chapter 4), and the subject matter for them is limitless. Basically, a suggestive pun is created when one symbol is used as a key symbol or when two or more symbols are combined to create one key symbol that can imply two or more meanings or associations. The multiple meanings or associations are applicable to the overall message, although they may differ widely. They are called "suggestive" because the pun is *not literal but suggested*. Depending on how the key symbol is used, it can bring appropriate associations to the message in new and witty ways. For instance, in one of Boston's WGBH-TV Channel 2 ads, the station number was substituted on the label of a prestigious perfume bottle, and the ad was run in one of Boston's fashion-conscious tabloids—a clever way to suggest similarities in quality and a taste for elegance to the same market.

Milton Glaser creates an affectionate
motto for New York City with this literal
pun.

The Comparative Pun. Different from the first two types, comparative puns rely on *at least two key symbols* to create the pun effect. In them, symbols that are visually similar are placed in similar situations for comparison. The basic methods of producing them are through substitution, manipulation, or some combination of the two. In addition, there is a reversal in the pun effect from that of the first two. Instead of always creating multiple meanings or associations, the comparative pun sometimes simply communicates that one image has replaced another. The effect remains a pun because the key symbols add something special to the mes-

By substituting WGBH-TV Boston's station number on the label of a prestigious perfume, Chris Pullman suggests that their qualities are one and the same. To further the impact and wit, the ad was run full page in a fashion-conscious Boston tabloid.

Eli Kince uses circular foods and blank spaces in place of the letter *o*'s in these two comparative-pun posters for Yale dining halls.

sage. For example, Eli Kince used a comparative pun technique in his dining hall poster series. In the first poster, round food and fruit were substituted for the letter *o* in the words. The poster was placed in Yale dining halls for a week. On the eighth day, the second poster with only spaces for the *o*'s was put up. The pun effect was created first with edibles and then with spaces. Both were used as key symbols, and both were appropriate and added impact to the message.

The Effect of Puns

The effect of visual puns and other forms of image play can be defined as a visual experience in which a discrepancy exists between what we see and the actual physical character of the original stimuli. This is possible because some symbols are able to trigger a variety of intellectual associations. Although some symbols are used to create a discrepancy in a humorous or comic fashion, many puns capitalize on the same technique for the purpose of serious or subtle symbolic associations. To differentiate the two basic types, let's call the first group the *humorous pun effect* and the latter the *analytical pun effect*.

To review our definition, a pun effect is achieved, whether it is humorous or analytical, when a viewer becomes aware that one or more symbols have multiple associations that are all applicable to one statement. The eyes "can't believe what they are seeing," and the mind tries to link the incompatible thoughts to the statement. For a moment, the pun creates an intellectual puzzle, and somewhere in between the short time when the viewer recognizes the possible associations and solves the puzzle, the message seeps into the unconscious. At the moment the viewer solves the pun's puzzle, there is either an emotional or intellectual release of tension in the form of smiles, laughter, groans, or other acts of recognition.

The Humorous Pun Effect. The pun effect is humorous when a certain sense of cleverness and surprise is created. That mental jolt creates a humorous "spark," which releases tension in the form of a smile or a laugh. The "Dracula" poster created by Rand Shuster (page 90) is a perfect example of the humorous pun effect cleverly at work in an effective communications piece. Dracula is famous for his fangs, Rand Shuster sees them in his name, and the fictional character comes to life.

The Analytical Pun Effect. The pun effect is analytical when symbols are used in witty and apt ways and are appreciated intellectually more than emotionally. Such a reaction is produced because the context in which a symbol is used or manipulated appeals more to a person's logical or analytical sense than to his or her emotional responses. For instance, the *Bull's Head* by Pablo Picasso (see page 26) is an analytical pun, created by the addition of a new association to common items: The play is just as much on the bull as on the bike, if not more so. It was created not to

leave you howling with laughter, or not even for any shock value beyond the initial impact, but for intellectual enjoyment. Another example, *Violon d'Ingres* by Man Ray (see page 24), is created in a slightly different way. Ray compares aspects of symbols that are on the fringes of our awareness. We intellectually perceive the possible application of the multiple associations.

The degree of satisfaction received from solving a pun can depend on its complexity of uniqueness. In some cases a pun's effectiveness can depend on the appropriateness of the solution, which can be very simple but just as pertinent as the more complex ones. Effectiveness becomes a matter of using the right symbols for the right messages. Once any symbol is altered to a noticeable degree, it can have an impact on the conscious, unconscious, or both, depending of course on the symbol, its usage, and the audience.

Puns and Mass Communication

Theoretically at least, the world is much smaller than it was 150 years ago, and information can reach many audiences at once. Mass communication can be more effective with the timely use of visual puns. At a glance, puns can provide a break in a complex and hectic day, a quick step outside the world of duty and responsibility. They are a useful tool for the graphic designer.

A word of caution is in order, however. When choosing among symbols, you must consider the diverse experiences of your audience. Puns reflect people's tastes, which are founded on education, class, and cultural awareness. Furthermore, the choice of symbols must be considered with the particular audience in mind. It is obvious that mass communication serves to inform as well as to entertain. But of many symbols available to pick and choose from, there are few universal enough to touch everyone or reach a sizable cross-section in any society. The Red Cross logo is one that can. The Red Cross logo has become an international symbol because of the work of the organization. The logo's simplicity makes it easily recognizable. Consequently, the commonness of this particular symbol creates a universality that enables it to transcend language and cultural barriers.

The examples of visual puns that follow in Chapters 3 through 5 are from the work of various artists and designers. Some of the puns are more successful than others, but all of them make use of visual symbols to suggest two or more meanings or associations in order to make the essence of the intended message more accessible, efficient, and memorable.

The Red Cross logo is able to communicate on an international level because the five squares that form the symbol are easily recognizable and because the institution's work is known throughout the world.

When the name
Picasso falls upon the eye, a portrait
of a legend comes to mind. It's the legend in the
world of art which surrounds a man who possessed and
expressed many of the highest ideals of mankind. The popular
legend is of the outward attributes: seclusion and gregariousness; wealth
and love; abundance of works and extraordinary versatility in all facets of his
field. It has been estimated that Picasso created over fifty thousand works of art. Pablo Ruiz Picasso was born into a family of art, so he naturally had a very early beginning
in his creations. His life was long, ninety-one years, but when we do the arithmetic we still find
that he averaged throughout his creative years almost two pieces of art per day. Considering the
physical size and the conceptual scope of many of his works, these numbers bespeak a remarkable feat.
How is it that a man could be so one-pointed and inventive that he would become, as one author describes
him,"the most prolific artist of all times?" Picasso's own words may reveal the answer: "Painting is stronger than I
am; also,"painting makes me do what it wants." Another of the components of the popular legend is that
of his departure from tradition. Picasso is known by many as having been instrumental in founding and energiz-
ing two new movements in art, cubism and surrealism; and to have inspired other movements including abstract art and pop art. His departure into cubism, which has become perhaps his best known realm, was
met at the time with ridicule and contempt. The general attitude of those who saw this new trend was, at
best, closer to endurement than to endearment. A very few had any awareness that in Picasso painting was giving birth to truly significant modes of seeing and expression. These few, and Picasso himself, might have argued that
his seemingly radical forms were logical outcomes or extensions of the traditions of painting thus far, or at least, of the spirit
of painting. That same unbounded energy of art that had explored so many obvious and subtle ways of seeing was, in this
twentieth-century Spaniard, continuing its exploration. The world has indeed marveled that so much of that energy was con-
centrated through the eye-hand of this one man. Those who have known Picasso and have written of him begin to reveal
the inner, mystical legend when they independently ascribe this superconductivity to his unceasing wonderment-a won-
derment born of innocence and openness that had no need to look through the tinted glasses of dogma. Indeed, as
his own cubist movement became intellectually structured and dogmatic, he left its mainstream. In doing this,
he kept himself in the main evolutionary stream of art itself, which adheres to principles of a more general
and interaccommodative nature. Picasso was thus free to draw upon the principles he had discovered in
several specific modes of painting to achieve an even more comprehensive vision. One needs to be careful
not to think that he mixed some of this style and some of that to achieve something new. His art grew from
within and manifested itself in the appearance of mixture. He elaborated, "Art is not the application
of a canon of beauty, but what the instinct and the brain can conceive independently of that canon. When you love a woman you don't take instruments to measure her body, you love her
with your desires." His ability to create independently of the numerous canons of beauty
was witnessed by Gertrude Stein, one of his earliest patrons, who said,"He alone among
painters did not set himself the problem of expressing truths which all the world can
see, but the truth which only he can see." This internal truth must have been operative when
Picasso painted his well-known portrait of Gertrude Stein, for without something of an inner vision
his reflections on the portrait would seem absolutely baffling. As the story goes, he made Miss
Stein sit eighty times for the portrait, and then he wiped out her face and substituted a face with
mask-like qualities. There were criticisms which he dismissed with "Everybody thinks that the portrait is not
like her, but never mind, in the end she will look like the portrait." Such a statement might seem impertinent, but it is hard to question his integrity, for his commitment to his work was absolute. Every work was born of desire and in deep concentration. Every work was
also born living its own life. A painting or sculpture or lithograph or whatever, would begin in impulse, in vague idea, in spirit. Then as art "made him do what
it wanted" it would evolve through the brush of its creator. Each stroke and each picture was an end, a breathing universe itself. Picasso seldom signed his works and never
named them. He also customarily refused to explain them. It is perceived that such acts might have put too definitive boundaries on the pieces, limiting the potential that con-
tinues to exist within them. A father gives his child his own autonomy, never acknowledging the moment he becomes adult and never saying to him this is the kind of person you are
or that is the kind of influence you have, because the child may become much more or may be seen to be much more. For similar reasons, one hesitates to write of the legend of Pablo
Picasso, i.e. for fear of severely limiting its fullness. Yet, even as the legend itself is found within the depths of the viewer's consciousness, so are these words found looking out of a piece of paper.

3 THE LITERAL PUN

There is no pretense about literal puns. Here visual play is directly on the message. The key symbols selected should create at least two meanings, and each of these must clearly reflect the original message. Unlike the other types of puns, there's never any disparity or conflict in the multiple meanings of this pun. A feeling of repetition is most often evoked.

Literal puns must be distinguished from visual translations of a message. Visual translations are merely accurate descriptions of a verbal message. Nothing more, nothing less. They transfer the message from one medium to another. A clear example is the one-line series illustrated on the next page. One continuous line is used to visually interpret the meaning of three different words. (For more examples of visual translations, see Chapter 6, No Pun Intended.)

How They Are Created

There are three basic ways to create literal puns. The first is by selecting key symbols that have an inherent double meaning, the second relies on creating key symbols by combining symbols, and the third is by manipulating the key symbols.

Selecting Symbols with an Inherent Double Meaning. Symbols with an inherent double meaning are those that are visually one thing, verbally another, like a rebus puzzle where the picture of a bee stands for the word *be* or an eye for *I*. This type of pun originated thousands of years ago when the first writing systems were developed. For example, the sentence, "I saw you," is easy to illustrate visually—with the symbol of an eye, a picture of a saw, and the letter U. There is no visual connection between the words and the images, but once spoken, the message communicates.

Combining. To combine symbols, you can select various parts, rearrange them, substitute elements, and superimpose them. How much a symbol may be altered depends on its initial legibility and familiarity. The process of combining can change the symbolic meaning through emphasis or context or draw new attention to ordinary subjects. For example, by superimposing a thermometer over a lighted cigarette, Kyösti Varis combined everyday symbols to create "Your Lifemeter"—for an analytical pun effect with an obvious, ominous message.

Manipulating. Reducing, enlarging, or distorting symbols through manipulation can enhance the character or quality of the message. But there's the trap of making a visual translation instead of a pun. The fine line between the two is that a pun *always* has two or more meanings that are all applicable. A good example is Charles Hively's print ad for a photo lab operator, which also relies on the analytical pun effect. Printing the letterforms *out of focus* really makes the message *clear*.

Paul Siesman used different sizes and weights of type to create an image of Picasso. The pun is that the words not only form the image, they actually relate the story of the man's life.

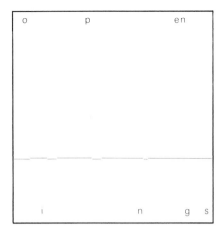

The Effects Created

The literal pun most effectively communicates ideas, feelings, and attitudes in simple, direct ways. Since the literal pun's message is basically blatant and doesn't require much imagination to interpret, it gets the most modest responses from cool and neutral *oh*'s to hesitant smiles to weak groans. Often the mild humor is created by a slight build-up in expectations and then a let-down effect. The very clever ones at the most are called "cute."

Most people respond that way to the literal pun because they think it is the most obvious choice; they instinctively understand that it couldn't have been complicated to produce. However, the simplest solutions are sometimes the most difficult to conceive.

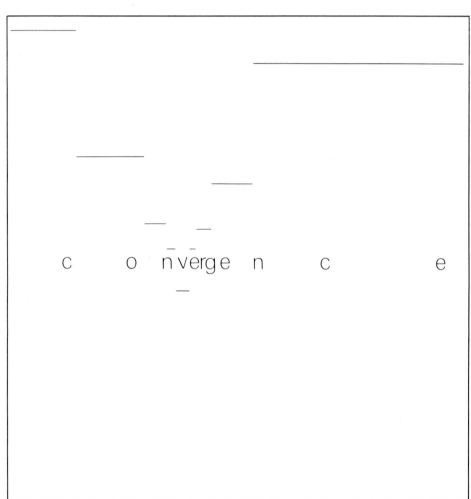

Typical of a visual translation, the line does what the word says.

"It's just a matter of time" is the poster's message. Here Kyösti Varis has chosen two unrelated symbols to state an old message in a fresh way.

We're looking for a sharp operator to work in our photo lab. Must have 24 years' experience and not be afraid of the dark. For a clearer picture, call Randy Ivey at Metzdorf Advertising. 526-5361. (We're an equal opportunity employer.)

Eli Kince created an image to suggest a brand for IBM's Quarter-Century Club annual dinner, which had a western theme.

The Allstate Insurance Companies symbol reflects their slogan, "You're in good hands with Allstate."

Obscuring the symbols, as Charles Hively did in this print ad, enhances the impact of the message.

This truck rental service uses the rebus principle in its name to distiguish it from movers.

An ampersand connects the letters *K* and *P* to form this literal logo for K&P stores in this design created by Millward & Millward, Inc.

One of the oldest pun techniques is
used here on a contemporary greeting
card by Sandra Boynton.

In this ad of a dog docilely holding a slipper, Bob Gill has used a stereotype in an inventive way.

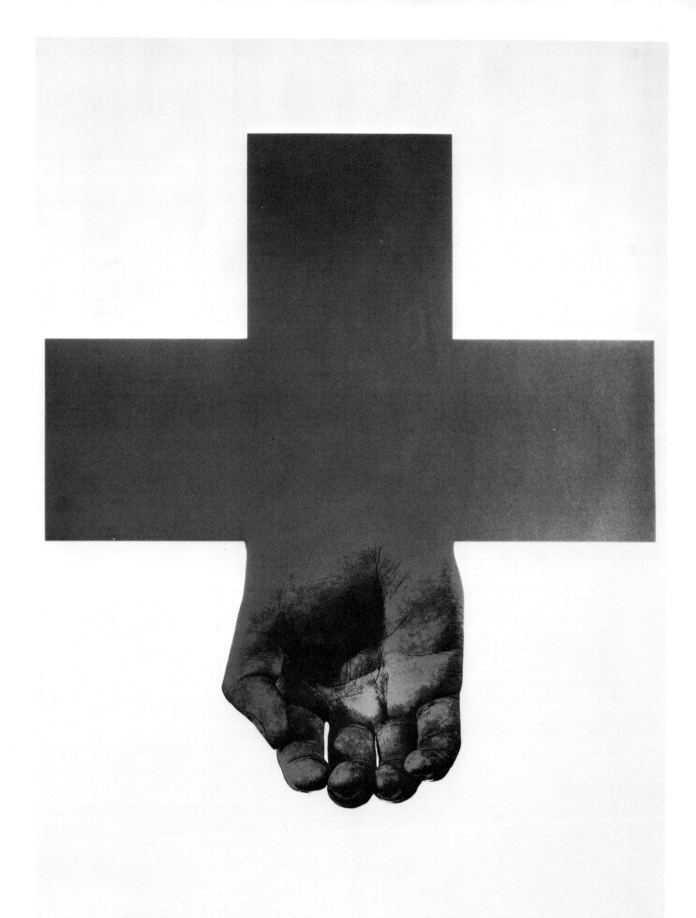

auta auttajia + help the helpers

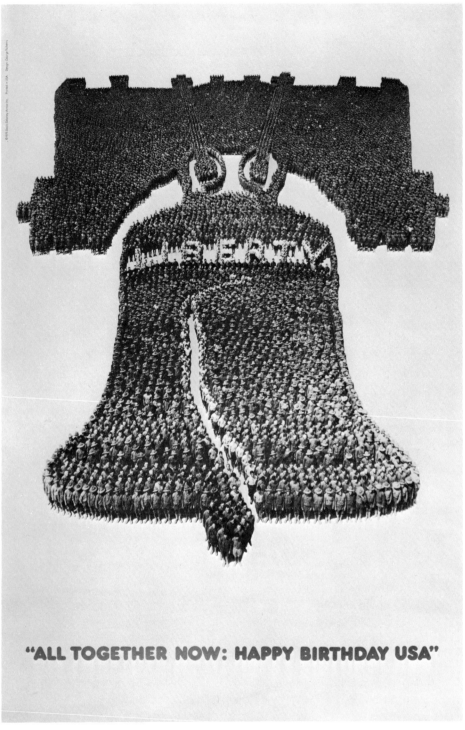

"ALL TOGETHER NOW: HAPPY BIRTHDAY USA"

Erkki Ruuhinen reinforces the essence of the Red Cross by adding a human hand to the symbol.

Without much alteration of the original symbols, Penguin Industries, Inc., cleverly combines the capital letter *P* with an image of a penguin to create the company's logo.

In the Liberty Bell poster for AT&T by George Tscherny, the overall silhouette is "read" first, with the people registering later. Tscherny believes that this "is because the eye takes in the overall shape before it focuses on detail, if it does at all."

THE LIBRARY IS FILLED WITH SUCCESS STORIES.

jaquette

The overall message is on the statement: "The library is filled with success
stories." The meaning becomes clear
from a combination of subtle symbols
and words.

Marcel Duchamp used an elegant cut-
away coat (in French, *jacquette*) for a
dust jacket of a book. He took the pun
further by showing the back of the coat
on the back.

For big babies.

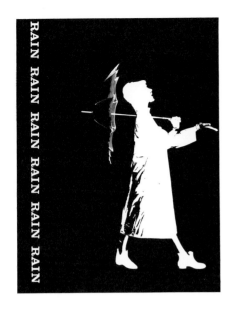

"Sunny and mild," says the weatherman. "Oh, yeah?" says the skeptic who lugs along an umbrella and brightens like a rainbow when rain starts to fall. The weather has frequently outsmarted the weatherman from the days of the first meteorologist, Theophrastus. This ancient Greek issued rain forecasts whenever he saw ducks diving in the harbor. Today's meteorologist, gathering his data from a network of government stations, supplies instruments and knowledge in order to predict upcoming weather. Scientific analysis is also employed in forecasting the business climate. Production, backlogs of orders, manufacturers' inventories, electric power output are some of the indicators which help the analyst to keep a weather-eye on the economic horizon. But business itself is spurred by a factor that doesn't fit into any chart or index. This is the dynamic vision which is created in business circles by ideas printed on paper. Graphic advertising enables the forward-looking businessman to see tomorrow's opportunities. If it rains today, he knows that sunny skies are sure to follow.

Photographs: Somoroff.
Magazine: Mademoiselle,
Publisher: Street & Smith Publications, Inc
Engravings: Line.

Printed by letterpress
on Sterling Letterpress Enamel,
25 x 38-80.

4195

In this poster for ASH (Action Against Smoking & Health) Ian James Wright combines symbols to suggest that smoking is a childish endeavor.

In this promotion piece for Westvaco by Bradbury Thompson, letters are strategically placed to suggest rain.

The Breaks
of the Game.

You couldn't resist that adorable little tennis dress. But how were you to know that when you attacked at the net, your zipper would be the one to surrender?

You should have made sure the dress had a zipper you could rely on. Like the Talon Zephyr® Nylon zipper. Its performance has been proven for

years on tennis courts all over the world.

That's why Talon is known as a quality zipper. And why it's your clue that the rest of the dress is well-made, too. The next time you buy a tennis dress (or any active sportswear), look for the Talon name.

Even if you have an undependable volley, at least you'll have a dependable zipper.

Talon

The Talon Zephyr Nylon Zipper says a lot about what it's in.

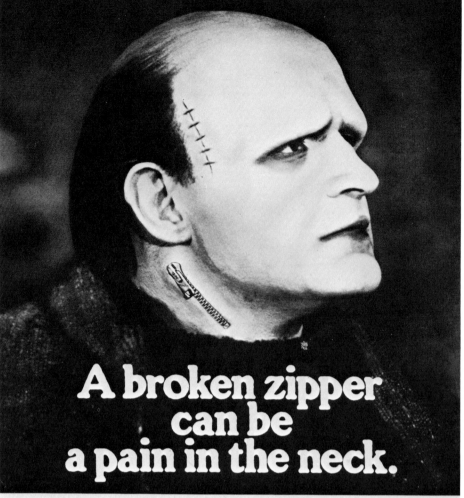

A broken zipper can be a pain in the neck.

When you're making something very strong, you have to hold it together with a zipper that's even stronger.

Like the Talon 42® metal zipper which was designed for strength.

We made it specifically for jeans and work pants, which means it's a zipper

that can take the roughest wear and endless washings.

The proof of its toughness is the way the Talon 42 has performed in millions and millions of jeans and work pants. (It also happens to be an excellent zipper for monsters.)

The next time you buy jeans, look for the Talon 42 zipper. It will tell you the manufacturer put as much care into his creation as Young Frankenstein put into his.

Talon
THE WORLD'S QUALITY ZIPPER

The Talon 42 zipper says a lot about the jeans it's in.

The series of ads for Talon zippers focuses on the embarrassing situations zippers can expose you to. Everyone can relate to the message.

Joseph Bottoni created a strong image in a poster for this famous Cincinnati fruit market by placing a map of it on an orange in a precise combination.

FINDLAY
MARKET

CINCINNATI'S HISTORICAL MARKET PLACE

Disappears rather quickly, doesn't it.

Give dad an expensive belt.

Showing only the bottle's label reinforces the Chivas Regal ad-copy message, as does the addition of the belt.

This billboard for Northwestern Bell is a
good example of how to position an advertisement to create a clear, direct,
memorable message.

Armin Hofmann creates a literal pun in German on house by reducing the R in BAUR so the BAU (*house* in German) is most prominent in this poster.

Design: Inge Druckrey

Friday October 12 1979 8:00 pm Woolsey Hall Admission free
Yale Symphony Orchestra

Robert Kapilow Music Director

Beethoven
Piano Concerto no. 5 "Emperor" C. Geanakoplos Soloist
Symphony no. 5

H   O   V   E   N

Inge Druckrey used linear elements and
letters to compose this musical poster
on Beethoven.

Photographer: Somoroff

On the retailer's shelf, the fast-moving package is the one with a colorful design that catches the

consumer's fancy. The manufacturer accelerates sales by restyling old products in new color.

The American home is brightened by exciting hues in everything from percale sheets to linoleum.

Commercial design borrows chromatic terms from the animal, vegetable and mineral realms;

motor-cars in robin's egg blue; plastic utensils in avocado green; fountain pens in turquoise blue.

Advertisers lure reading attention eye-compelling power of illustration and design in color.

When the consumer's eye nibbles at an idea in color the odds are heavy that a sale will be landed.

Use color for bait. Use color for bait. Use color for bait. Use color for bait. Use color for bait

J

Printed by letterpress on West Virginia Machine Coated, 25 x 38 - 70

Photographer: Newman-Schmidt Studios
Art Director: Tom Ross
Advertiser: Hagan Corporation,
Agency: Ketchum, MacLeod & Grove, Inc.
Engraving: Halftone engraving, 120 line screen   3535

4
THE SUGGESTIVE PUN

Suggestive puns are the visual counterparts of verbal semantic puns—when *red* is used to mean *read*. (See the American Library Association poster on the next page.) Instead of using one word to suggest, signify, or imply a second meaning, you use one image. This type of pun is called "suggestive" because it relies on one key symbol or two or more symbols combined to create a new key symbol that can suggest two or more meanings or associations at the same time. The multiple meanings may differ widely but each is appropriate to the overall statement. The suggestive pun is easy to identify because attention is focused on the possible interpretations of one key symbol.

In a suggestive pun, the key symbol can be visually tailored—that is, it can be altered by substitution, manipulation, or a combination of both techniques to create meanings that can either reinforce one another or present opposing views: similarity or disparity, concord or conflict. If there is just one symbol, it must occupy two separate spaces, two worlds, or two realities at the same time. And all the meanings are needed to create the overall message. Suggestive puns allow the designer an enormous freedom of expression, which accounts for the pun's popularity and wide use today.

How They Are Created

Suggestive puns can be created in two ways. The first is by selecting one key symbol and creating multiple meanings through association with the original or most obvious symbolic meaning. The second is by combining two or more key symbols to create a new symbol that can suggest or be many things at the same time. In either case, the multiple meanings must be able to bring additional information to the overall statement.

Association. Association can be defined further by breaking it down into five categories: relying on past experience, playing with expectations, substituting a similar symbol, manipulating the symbol, and combining parts of a symbol in a new or unique way.

Relying on Past Experiences. In the purest use of relying on past experiences, there is no alteration of the original image or words; the pun depends on how the key symbol is used to create the dual meaning. Often this method of punning is used for television commercials or product packaging or slogans because it does communicate clearly and is an effective way to tell two stories at once. A good example is the Alcoa Can and Bottling Company theme, "Many Happy Returns." The company has been actively advocating the recycling of aluminum cans for a decade, yet one of their more recent commercials shows that the company's concern goes beyond preventing environmental pollution. There is also an emphasis on rewarding public service. The two children in the ad get money for their good deed. But they also keep returning to the store to buy more products in aluminum cans.

In this promotion piece for Westvaco, Bradbury Thompson suggests water with two techniques: each line of the copy is surrounded by a gradually increasing amount of space and *o*'s of different sizes are randomly spaced to convey air bubbles. The main theme—"Use color for bait"—is printed in bright colors.

Stills selected from an Alcoa Can and Bottling Company television commercial show how a familiar greeting can be used in an innovative way.

One of a series of American Library Association posters that encourages people to use libraries, this poster plays with the phonetic similarity of the words *red* and *read*.

Playing with Expectations. Variety, excitement, surprise can be created by altering what the viewer is used to. So the key symbol here needs to be a very familiar one. One example of this type is the way WGBH-TV Channel 2 in Boston, the public service station, uses its station number 2. Chermayeff and Geismar—called in to develop a marketing concept for the station in 1973—suggested using a three-dimensional version of the 2 in various applications. Vaguely anthropomorphic, the number has proved to be a malleable character, portraying seasons, holidays, different programs, and locations in the Boston area, all with a change of costume or context (see series on next page). The various manifestations are suggestive puns because other elements are added to or subtracted from the basic shape to create a new and different message. Better than any rigid corporate logo, the versatile 2 has helped to identify the eclectic and somewhat unorthodox personality of this station and its programming, with both humorous and analytical pun effects.

Substitution. One of the purest forms of punning, substitution consists of replacing a word or image with another one. Appearance, then, is most important here. An example is how L'eggs, makers of pantyhose, worked their product name into a very effective ad campaign—"Nothing beats a great pair of L'eggs." Although the spelling is different, the sound and appearance of the word reinforce the message.

Nothing beats a great pair of L'eggs™

Manipulation. A suggestive pun allows the designer more freedom in positioning, enlarging, or repeating a key symbol through manipulation than a literal pun does because the second meaning does not have to reinforce the original message. It can create a different meaning or be just a smart graphic statement. For instance, on page 100 is a New Year's greeting by Advertising Designers, which shows how new life can be brought to an old message. The seemingly obvious manipulation of type creates a mood as fresh as a new snowfall.

Combining. Combining symbols to create suggestive puns also allows greater freedom than with literal puns because the second meaning does not have to be repetitive. In fact, it can raise a range of new meanings from the pragmatic to the playful. Often the symbols are combined in such a way that their message outweighs the means used to produce it. A new awareness is the result. Such is the case with Picasso's *Bull's Head* (shown on page 26). By creating the head from the seat and handle bars of a bicycle, Picasso makes a statement about a bull that is much stronger than the original bicycle parts.

The L'eggs slogan is a marketing strategy both clever and appropriate for its product.

About
the House

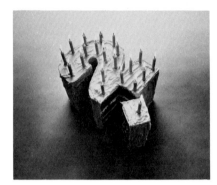

Applications of the three-dimensional 2
for WGBH-TV's program promotion are
enhanced by the varied materials selected to create the symbol and by the
way the symbol is placed in a diversity
of settings.

Combining to Form a New Key Symbol. A second method of creating suggestive puns is by combining two or more key symbols to create a new symbol that can suggest or be many things at the same time, with all meanings applicable. Lance Wyman's directional arrow for the Minnesota Zoo is an excellent example. In its combination of a bird with an arrow, the arrow is enhanced and probably becomes more legible because of its witty association with the bird. It's also very compatible with the environment for which it was designed. In this instance, there is a close conceptual union, unlike that of Picasso's bike and bull.

The Effects Created

Designers can take greater chances in communicating complex ideas, concepts, and feelings with suggestive puns than with other types. They can also create moods and atmospheres in which to air their messages. There is a certain amount of impact inherent in this category of puns because of the paradoxical situation created by one symbol or a combination of two or more appearing as one image but conveying two or more applicable meanings. We are almost immediately able to identify the one meaning; the second one is the surprise that creates the pun effect.

Unlike the literal pun that can only use the double meaning as a form of repetition, suggestive puns can be not only repetitive, but also offer a variety of different meanings, and even express opposing or conflicting views. As a result the viewer is often stimulated by unexpected unions of disparate meanings, all of which augment the overall message. Such is the case with Rand Shuster's logo for the movie "Dracula" (see page 90) and with WGBH-TV's promotional series. The former plays with specific information—the teeth—in a way that seems menacingly new each time you see it, while the latter plays with a key symbol to communicate unexpected concepts, feelings, and moods. There is no limit to the symbols from which you can select to enhance or create a message. Picasso created a bull's head from bicycle parts. What was his message? The bicycle or the bull's head?

The humorous pun effect is often found in suggestive puns. The sudden surprise or witty interpretation of symbols and their meanings many times evokes a smile or even laughter. The best test to assess if a suggestive pun is successful is not to see it for a while. If the original reaction returns, you know it is. There is in this category of puns, a certain magic, that comes from a quick, spontaneous appreciation of both its methods and its message.

Lance Wyman's directional arrow for the Minnesota Zoo unites an arrow and a bird in one appropriate symbol. An additional meaning is the suggestion of movement.

Rudolph de Harak used a stylized wavy line to suggest both sound waves and mountains on this book jacket.

In a student project assigned at the Parsons School of Design in New York, Orietta Arroyo created this logo for the Barbershop Quartet, with a succinct combination of a moustache and musical notes.

Bruce Blackburn (while working for
Chermayeff & Geismar Associates)
used black and white circles to illustrate different topics in this Atheneum
book series on the various historical
roles of Black people in the Western
Hemisphere.

McGraw-Hill Paperbacks

Stanford University Press

The Siege of Leningrad
Leon Goure
Foreword by Merle Fainsod

Rudolph deHarak

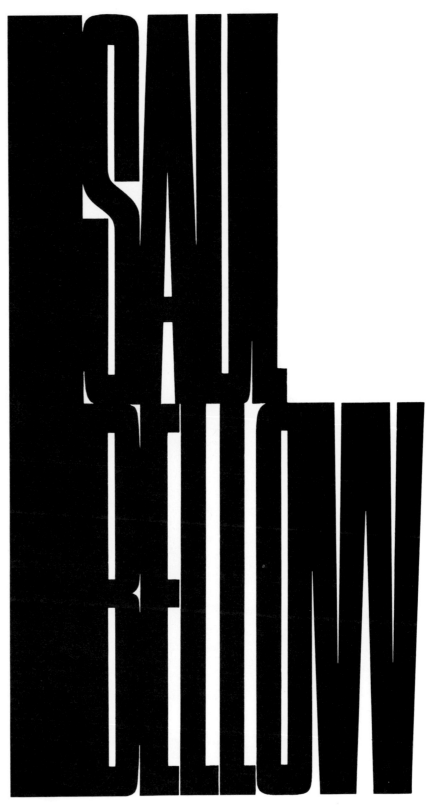

On this book jacket Rudolph De Harak combines two symbols so efficiently that the message of an invasion cannot be mistaken.

Peter Millward creates a play on the subject's name by condensing the letterforms to suggest an unextended bellows and the capital letter *L*.

Pray
for
Rosemary's
Baby

The Playboy logo, which plays on the proclivities of a particular animal, has become familiar around the world.

In a poster promoting the film ''Rosemary's Baby,'' Danne & Blackburn suggest an umbilical cord connecting mother and child.

MOTHER
(CHILD)

Families
A READER'S DIGEST
PUBLICATION

Herb Lubalin created these successful
logos by manipulating the letterforms to
suggest the meanings of the particular
words. While the solutions appear obvious, they are actually difficult to conceive.

Pentagram combines fantasy with reality in this Pirelli slipper ad. The constantly changing clientele of the bus give a humorous impact to the billboard.

A

BC

DEF

GHIJK

LMNOP

QRSTU

VWXYZ

1 2 3 4 5

6 7 8 9 0

CLARENDON

WEST VIRGINIA PULP AND PAPER COMPANY

By arranging the letterforms and numerals of the Clarendon typeface to resemble an eye chart, Bradbury Thompson creates a subtle pun for a Westvaco promotion piece. The pun effect is enhanced by the placement of the point size next to each row.

Eli Kince suggests a construction site by an adroit placement of words.

Product
of the mind.

Profitable wine brands share one important
characteristic. The consumer perceives their value
in his mind.

Experience has taught us, it is not what's in
the bottle but what's in the mind...that builds
profitable brands.

TIME, too, is a product of the mind—
a thoughtful editorial environment provoking
interest in what is new and what is news. It
provides the wine advertiser an unmatched background for brand recognition and appreciation.

TIME has always broadened the awareness
of its readers. That's why, ever since Americans
first discovered the glories of the grape, wine
advertisers have chosen TIME to enhance the
awareness of their brands.

Think about it.

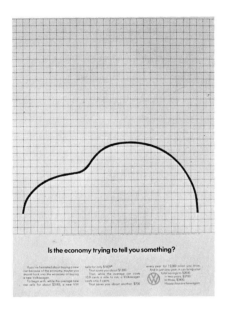

Is the economy trying to tell you something?

Lemon.

This Volkswagen missed the boat.

The chrome strip on the glove compartment is blemished and must be replaced. Chances are you wouldn't have noticed it; Inspector Kurt Kroner did.

There are 3,389 men at our Wolfsburg factory with only one job: to inspect Volkswagens at each stage of production. (3000 Volkswagens are produced daily; there are more inspectors than cars.)

Every shock absorber is tested (spot checking won't do), every windshield is scanned. VWs have been rejected for surface scratches barely visible to the eye.

Final inspection is really something! VW inspectors run each car off the line onto the Funktionsprüfstand (car test stand), tote up 189 check points, gun ahead to the automatic brake stand, and say "no" to one VW out of fifty.

This preoccupation with detail means the VW lasts longer and requires less maintenance, by and large, than other cars. (It also means a used VW depreciates less than any other car.)

We pluck the lemons; you get the plums.

Time's ad campaign cleverly communicates with substitution. Designed by Young & Rubicam, the ads rely on the audience's familiarity with the name and type style of the magazine's title.

The Doyle Dane Bernbach ad campaign for Volkswagon, begun in 1959, brought fresh, challenging humor to the advertising world. While making fun of the product, the campaign capitalizes on the VW's unchanging appearance and the audience's preconceived ideas about the car.

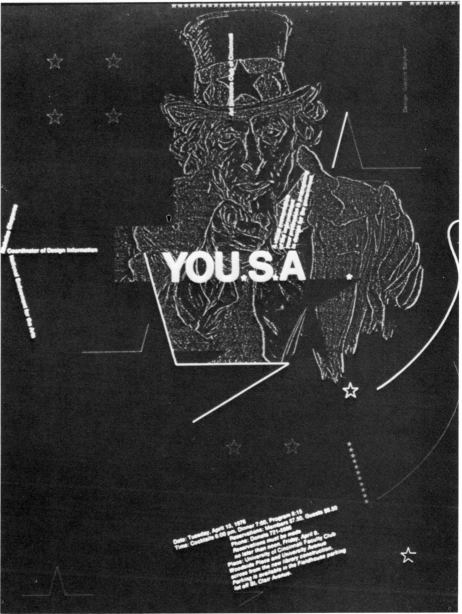

The pun effect is set up by the headline in this ad created by the Scali, McCabe, Sloves agency for the Metropolitan Opera. While one interpretation may be an invitation to join the cast, the other cleverly requests donations.

In this poster advertising visiting speakers, Gordon Salchow, through exaggeration, attacks the current fad for displaying designers' signatures.

Gordon Salchow uses a reverse rebus to recruit designers with this poster for the Federal Design Improvement Program sponsored by the National Endowment for the Arts. By substituting a personal pronoun for a collective term, Salchow gives the message impact.

The feeling of Egypt is conveyed in this illustration series by Eli Kince. Links from an Egyptian necklace and triangular letterforms suggesting the pyramids are the key symbols.

Dan Reisinger creates a powerful suggestive pun by substituting a hammer and sickle for the *G* in this poster.

DRACULA

FRIDAY THE 13TH DRACULA, DIRECTED BY RONALD WILLE
FEBRUARY 13, 14, 20, 21, 8:00 PM, 15 & 22, 2:30 PM
FINE ARTS AUDITORIUM, NCCC, SPONSORED BY THE THEATRE
ARTS DEPARTMENT AND THE STUDENT SENATE
TICKETS $2.00, SENIOR CITIZEN $1.00, NCCC STUDENTS FREE

DESIGNED BY RAND SCHUSTER   NCCC

desi8n 63

Rand Schuster's poster brings Dracula's name to life with a flop of the two a's

In a promotion piece for an annual exhibition, Paul Rand's 8 serves two functions: one as the letter g and the other as an identifier of the eighth annual event.

Did you hear the one about the 3rd World War?

Knock knock.

Who's there?

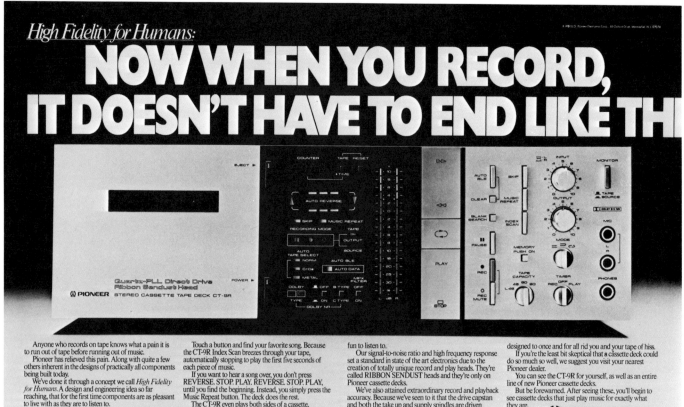

High Fidelity for Humans:

NOW WHEN YOU RECORD, IT DOESN'T HAVE TO END LIKE THI

Anyone who records on tape knows what a pain it is to run out of tape before running out of music.

Pioneer has relieved this pain. Along with quite a few others inherent in the designs of practically all components being built today.

We've done it through a concept we call *High Fidelity for Humans.* A design and engineering idea so far reaching, that for the first time components are as pleasant to live with as they are to listen to.

For example, our new CT-9R cassette deck shows you a digital readout of the precise amount of recording time left on a tape.

Touch a button and find your favorite song. Because the CT-9R Index Scan breezes through your tape, automatically stopping to play the first five seconds of each piece of music.

If you want to hear a song over, you don't press REVERSE. STOP. PLAY. REVERSE. STOP. PLAY, until you find the beginning. Instead, you simply press the Music Repeat button. The deck does the rest.

The CT-9R even plays both sides of a cassette, automatically.

But don't get the idea that we've produced a cassette deck that is just a lot of fun to play with. It's also a lot of

fun to listen to.

Our signal-to-noise ratio and high frequency response set a standard in state of the art electronics due to the creation of totally unique record and play heads. They're called RIBBON SENDUST heads and they're only on Pioneer cassette decks.

We've also attained extraordinary record and playback accuracy. Because we've seen to it that the drive capstan and both the take up and supply spindles are driven directly by their own motors. We call it our 3 Direct Drive motor transport and it, too, is exclusively Pioneer's.

Plus, we have Dolby C. The latest in Dolby engineering,

designed to once and for all rid you and your tape of hiss.

If you're the least bit skeptical that a cassette deck could do so much so well, we suggest you visit your nearest Pioneer dealer.

You can see the CT-9R for yourself, as well as an entire line of new Pioneer cassette decks.

But be forewarned. After seeing these, you'll begin to see cassette decks that just play music for exactly what they are.

Somewhat less than adequate.

⦿ PIONEER
We bring it back alive.

Verbal play is translated into visual play, with both methods used to make a strong message in this poster by Tony Palladino.

In this ad for Pioneer, part of the word *this* is cut off to literally reinforce the message.

Bob Gill uses substitution in the logo for Television Automation to create a clear and concise image.

In this birthday greeting from CBS to NBC, Lou Dorfsman used substitution to create the pun effect.

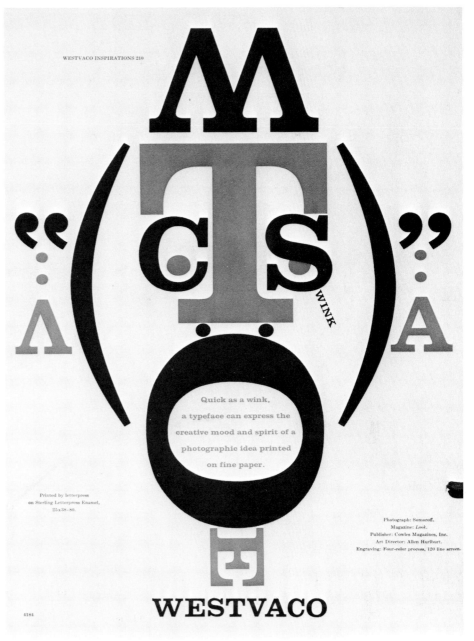

WINK

Quick as a wink,
a typeface can express the
creative mood and spirit of a
photographic idea printed
on fine paper.

Printed by letterpress
on Sterling Letterpress Enamel,
25x38-80.

Photograph: Somoroff.
Magazine: *Look.*
Publisher: Cowles Magazines, Inc.
Art Director: Allen Hurlburt.
Engraving: Four-color process, 120 line screen.

4184

WESTVACO

Jerry Pinkney combines visual symbols in this unpublished illustration for a magazine article entitled ''Love, Sex, and the Blues.'' The main theme of the article is about the hardships of a female vocalist who sang the blues.

In this promotion piece for Westvaco, Bradbury Thompson makes the letter-forms come to life in this African mask.

Pentagram takes a common carpenter's joint and substitutes it for the counterspace of the letter p to create an effective and provocative logo for Pevsner, a London carpenter.

Suggesting both the water and the fish, this logo was created by Chermayeff & Geismar Associates for the Baltimore Aquarium.

Composed of fruits and vegetables, *Portrait of Rudolf II as Vertumnus* was one of many pictures Arcimboldo painted while developing his composite portrait style.

Arcimboldo arranged books to create this composite portrait of *The Librarian*.

PAINTED
SCULPTURE

Painted Sculpture artists:

Charles Arnoldi
David Bottini
Linda Fleming
Robert Hudson

Roy Lichtenstein
John McCracken
Manuel Neri
George Page
Harold Paris

Jay Phillips
Sam Richardson
Kent Roberts
Joseph Slusky
Elisabeth Munro Smith

Ann Sperry
Frank Stella
Michael Stevens
George Sugarman
Gerald Walburg

AUGUST 31 - OCTOBER 26, 1980   PALO ALTO CULTURAL CENTER

Design: Russell Leong Design Group

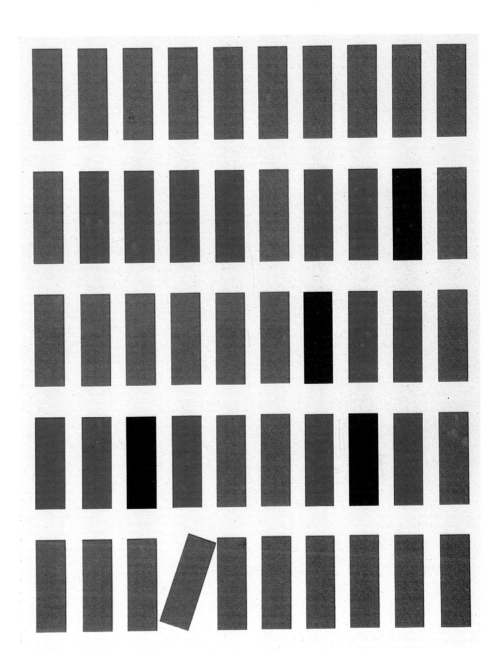

The Palo Alto Cultural Center poster created by Russell Leong suggests multimedia in a provocative manner.

Paul Rand's design of a folder for the American Institute of Graphic Arts show of the 50 best books of the year proves that "the effectiveness of a design is often dependent upon a small, visual clue."

Our way of wishing you a Happy-type New Year. Stop in and we'll give you a snow job. Any time. ADVERTISING DESIGNERS, INC. 818 North La Brea 90 038

In this self-promotion piece for Advertising Designers, the reverse type positioned as snow flakes convincingly communicates a delicate snowfall. Carl Seltzer and Tom Ohmer were responsible for this snow job.

In this poster by Bertil Strandell, the human body is manipulated to enact the theme: "Reading is to the mind as gymnastics is to the body."

Oktober 1971   Fr Lö Sö Må Ti On To Fr Lö Sö Må Ti On To Fr Lö Sö Må Ti On To Fr Lö Sö Må Ti On To Fr Lö Sö
                1 2 3 4 5 6 7 8 9 10 11 12 13 14 15 16 17 18 19 20 21 22 23 24 25 26 27 28 29 30 31

Detta är en tolftedel av en årskalender från Ateljé von Sterneck och Hedmans Repro AB.

Läsning är för själen vad gymnastik är för kroppen.

ABC-TV's subway poster, advertising its local New York City Eye-Witness News team, relies on a series of three side-by-side posters with their midsections seemingly ripped away. The pun is created by the juxtaposition of torn images and the usual appearance of the environment in which they were placed.

In a manner similar to that in ABC-TV's series of advertisements, Levi Strauss takes advantage of the nature of billboard advertising and of its own past campaigns to make this new and provocative statement.

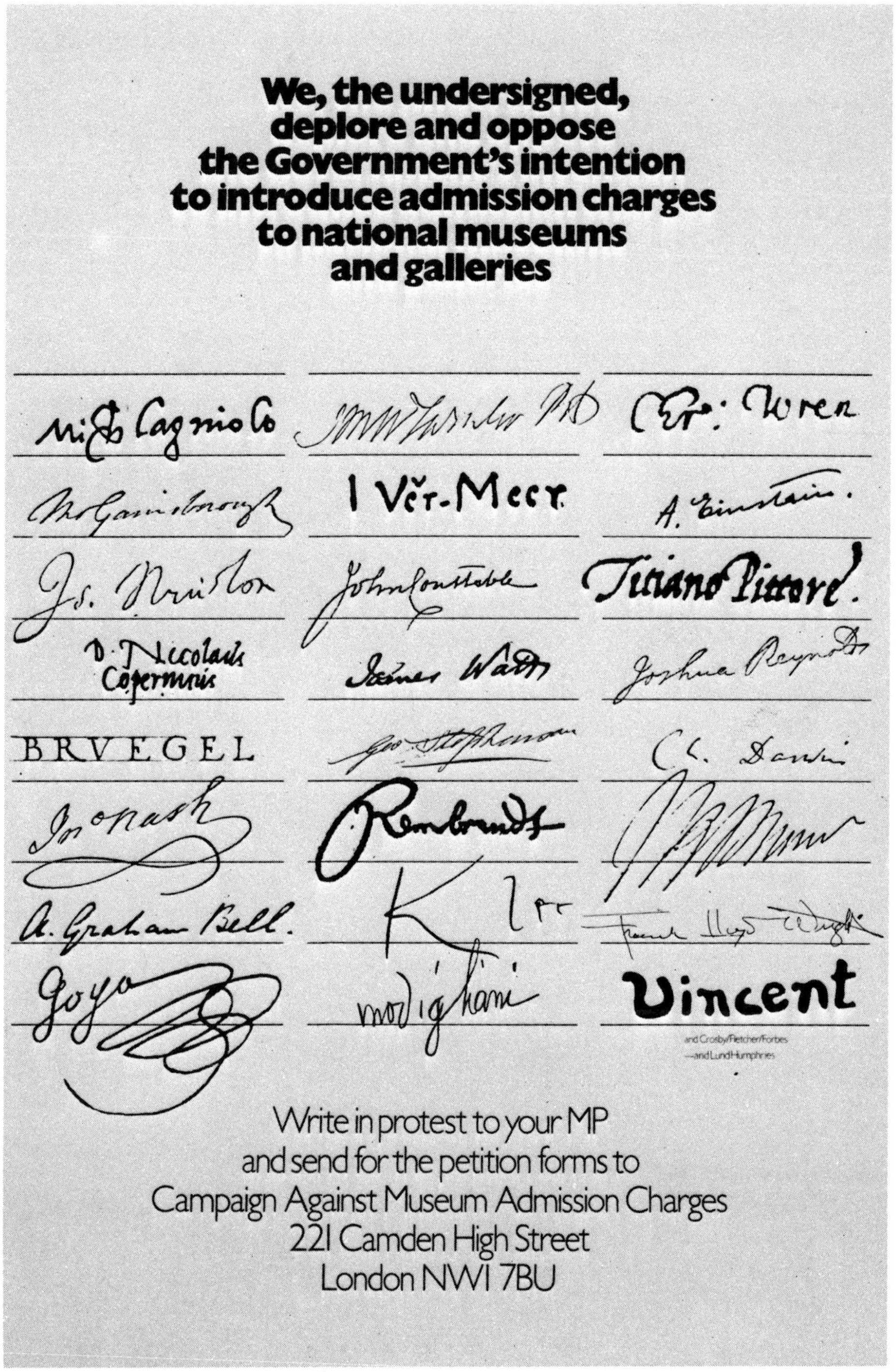

We, the undersigned, deplore and oppose the Government's intention to introduce admission charges to national museums and galleries
I Ver-Meer
BRVEGEL
Rembrandt
Vincent
and Crosby/Fletcher/Forbes
—and Lund Humphries
Write in protest to your MP
and send for the petition forms to
Campaign Against Museum Admission Charges
221 Camden High Street
London NW1 7BU

Greg Brown has created a deceptive painting of a night deposit box for the University National Bank in Palo Alto, California.

The poster by Pentagram brings the masters to life while making an effective statement.

Boston
a new national park...

Boston National Historical Park: Faneuil Hall   Old South Meeting House   National Park Service
                                   Paul Revere House   Old State House   U.S. Department of the Interior
                                   Old North Church   Bunker Hill
                                   Charlestown Navy Yard

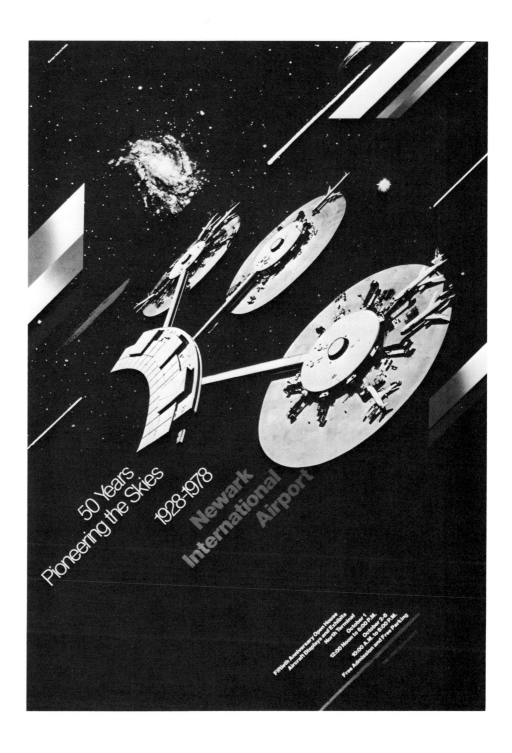

In this poster announcing Boston as a new National Historical Park, Paul Rand combines a stylized image, which can be interpreted as either a person or a star; a torch for freedom, which recalls the Statue of Liberty; and confetti, which conveys a celebration.

Valerie Pettis imagines that an airport is really a space ship in this poster for the New York Port Authority.

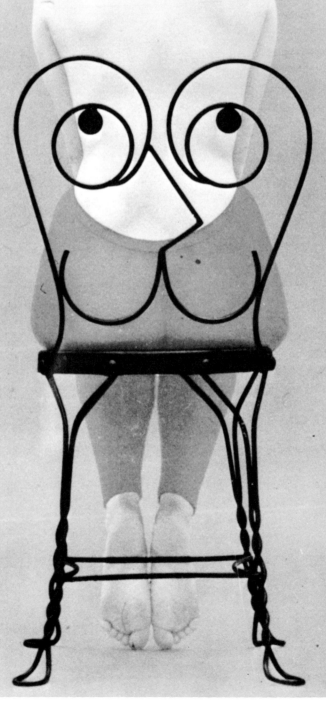

Women in Design: The next decade—A conference for women who work with public visual and physical forms, March 20th at the Woman's Building, 1727 North Spring Street, Los Angeles, California 90012.

Reminiscent of Man Ray's illustration *Violon d'Ingres*, Henry Wolf's *Esquire* cover combines a woman's back with a wire chair to suggest a face.

By using a standard design convention of determining space and perspective, Sheila Levrant deBretteville combines screws and nuts to make the woman's symbol in this poster for the Women in Design Conference. With the symbols positioned few and far between, the overall image suggests that women are not getting a fair share of opportunity and respect in the design field.

GUGGENHEIM MUSEUM OPEN FREE TUESDAY EVENINGS

89th St & 5th Ave
5 to 8 pm
Made possible
by a grant from Mobil

Basler Freilichtspiele
beim Letziturm im St. Albantal
15.-31. VIII 1963

Wilhelm Tell

This poster created by Chermayeff &
Geismar Associates for the Guggen-
heim Museum capitalizes on the most
visible trait of the building.

Armin Hofmann recreates the tale of
William Tell in this poster, with Tell's
surname functioning as the arrow.

George Tscherny assembled airplanes
in the configuration of a snowflake in a
poster / Christmas card for Overseas
National Airways.

By arranging paper clips into an organizational pyramid—the traditional symbol of a corporate chain of command—Pentagram creates a memorable book jacket.

The thumbprint with manipulated
arches, loops, and whorls identifies the
popular singing group Chicago. The
group always features its name as the
main graphic on its album covers.

Because of the eloquent simplicity of style in this logo, designed by Lance Wyman for the Minnesota Zoo, both the moose and the *M* are legible. This is an excellent example of maintaining the integrity of symbols, as are the animation of numerals indicating corresponding areas in the zoo.

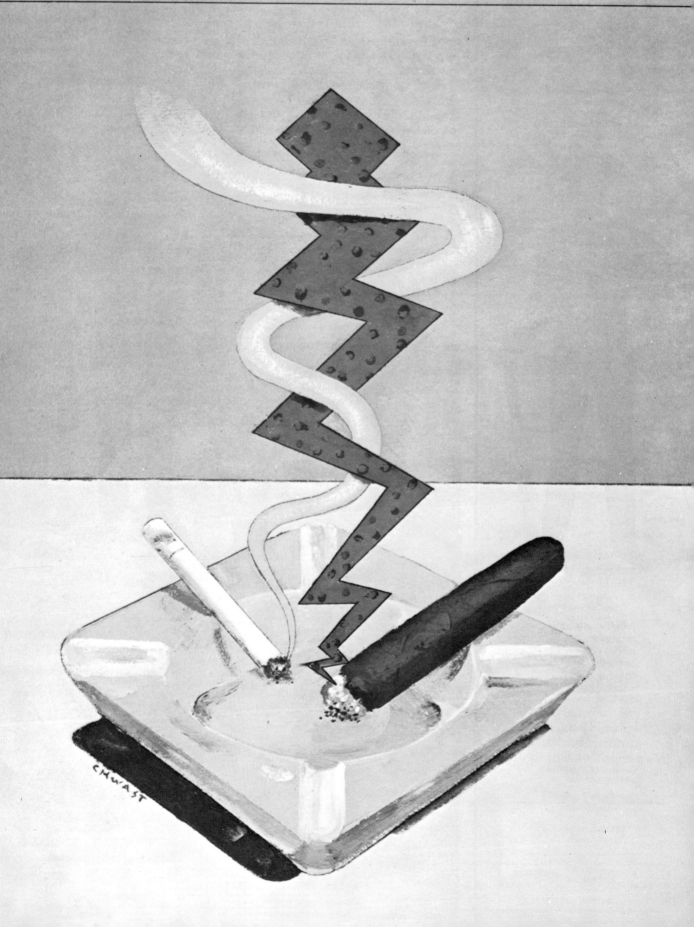

Comparative puns have their roots in homonymic word play in which the same word is used twice, as in "To England will I steal, and there I'll steal" (from Shakespeare's *Henry V*). In comparative puns, two or more symbols of the same or nearly the same appearance are compared, or the same symbol is juxtaposed two or more times, with the key symbols selected to enhance the overall statement. Since the names for literal and suggestive puns clearly define the function of their respective symbols, so too with this category. The pun is created by the process of the comparison, which produces an additional meaning or a new interpretation for the pun effect.

How They Are Created

Quite different in structure from literal and suggestive puns, comparative puns rely strongly on substitution. They are also created by manipulation, as well as by a combination of the substitution and manipulation techniques.

Substitution. Adding or subtracting two key symbols with similar appearance is the essence of substitution. The only difference from substitution in suggestive puns is that here *two similar images in similar situations* set up the pun effect. For instance, in his poster "Rock and Roll," shown on the next page, Herb Lubalin subtracted the letter *o* from both words and substituted the first with a real rock and the second with a bread roll. While the original meanings of these two words are incidentally reinforced, the overall message is given a new twist.

Manipulation. As with literal and suggestive puns, positioning, enlarging, reducing, or distorting key symbols is a way to create a comparative pun. Here too there's more freedom than with literal puns because the original message doesn't have to be repeated. The only requirement is that there be two key symbols. A good example is Seymour Chwast's illustration for the cover of *Push Pin* magazine. Arising from an ashtray are two kinds of smoke: that from a cigarette is misty, flowing, and delicate because of rounded edges and soft curves, while that from a cigar is jagged, sharp, and bold, like a lightning bolt. In further contrast, the cigarette smoke is pale and monochromatic, while the cigar smoke is filled with bold and vivid color. There is no type on the cover to identify the illustration, but the lipstick on the cigarette is another symbol that indicates this is a statement about couples. Once you identify it, the message is hard to forget.

Combining. A great range of expression, as well as the possibility of subtlety, is allowed by combining substitution and manipulation of two key symbols. Paul Rand exercises that option in his poster for the 1982 Aspen Design Conference. By positioning two red targets on a black field, Rand uses bullet holes to communicate his message. The subtlety is that the target on the right has a bull's eye, which is not at first apparent, while the one on the left has been barraged with random bullets. In this instance,

Seymour Chwast manipulates line and color to create this comparative pun used on the cover of *Push Pin* magazine to illustrate an issue on couples.

Ever since a
ROCK
was a stone
and a
ROLL
was a bun...

the symbols used to create the message are not obvious. The process of discovering the symbols and understanding their message through association in this particular context is what makes this an effective pun.

The Effects Created

A designer must know the range of possibilities of symbols and what they convey when creating puns, but especially when making comparative puns. They have the potential of being the most memorable of the three types, but that depends on how skillfully they are controlled. Selecting symbols that can interact and play off each other when placed together is the art. By being sensitive to how people react to various symbols, both intellectually and intuitively, the designer can create a precise image with a lasting message.

If you react to one element that practically shouts out from a visual pun, you've probably located the key symbol. That is particularly true of suggestive puns. However, comparative puns can be more difficult to identify because of the subtlety of the comparison between the elements. That may account for the neutral turf that comparative puns seem to occupy emotionally. While they can be humorous, as in Lubalin's "Rock and Roll," or didactic, like Rand's poster, they seldom offend because of a personal bias, nor can they be dismissed as stereotypical. At worst, they appear predictable, triggering that part of the subconscious that makes you think you could have done the same thing with little effort. However, that is their beauty. They seem to touch an intuitive sense in everyone. That association is what makes their effect long lasting.

Since intuition is often rejected in this society in favor of intellect, there isn't an abundance of comparative puns. With an awareness of their impact, however, designers should consider their powerful potential.

In this design for a poster, Herb Lubalin substitutes a rock and a roll to give the title a new twist.

Paul Rand's message is on target in this simple, yet powerful poster for the Aspen Design Conference.

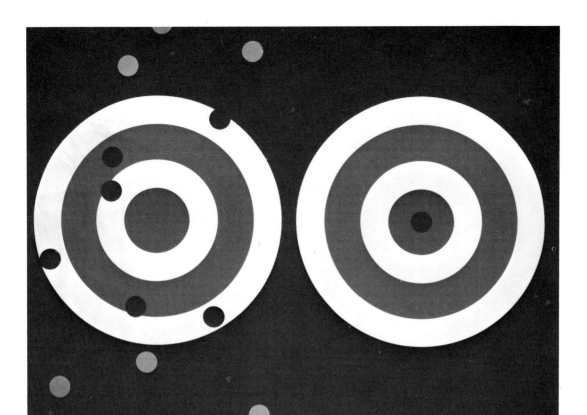

The
Prepared
Professional

International
Design Conference
in Aspen
June 13–18, '82

As modern society moves from the earlier dominance of
agriculture and industry into its tertiary or cybernetic phase,
the role of the professional becomes central.
Old questions take on new meanings.
How is the professional prepared?
What, in a fast-changing scene, should he prepare for?
How do roles and responsibilities change?
What happens to the traditional values of the professional?
How does he adapt to the pressures of a mass society?
What kind of future does he look forward to?

Registration Fees: (U.S. Dollars) $300. One Additional Member of Household
$150; Full Time Student (xerox of current student ID required with application) $125.
List all applicants by name, and make check payable to IDCA and mail with
registration to: IDCA c/o The Bank of Aspen, P.O. Box O, Aspen, Colorado 81612.
(Your canceled check is your confirmation.)

Housing and Travel: Aspen Ski Tours, 300 South Spring Street, Aspen,
Colorado 81611 (303 925 4526) and/or Aspen Central Reservations, 700 South
Aspen Street, Aspen, Colorado 81611 (303 925 9000).

Camping Information: U.S. Forest Service, 806 West Hallum, Aspen, Colorado 81611.

Additional Information: IDCA, P.O. Box 664, Aspen, Colorado 81612
(303 925 2257 or 303 925 6265).

In this advertisement for a paper company, Bob Gill uses the same piece of paper to make a comparative pun.

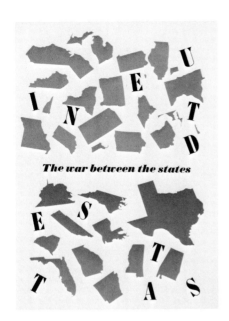

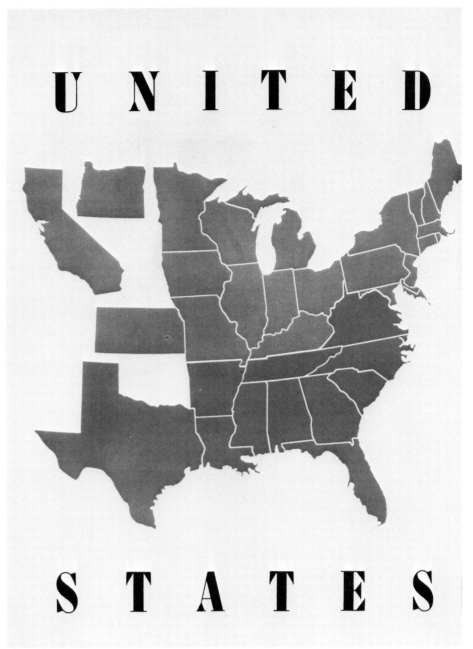

Bradbury Thompson created a two-part
literal pun when he designed this book-
divider page. The message does not
pull together until the images do.

To the executives and management of the Radio Corporation of America:

Messrs. Alexander, Anderson, Baker, Buck, Cahill, Cannon, Carter, Coe, Coffin, Dunlap, Elliott, Engstrom, Folsom, Gorin, Jolliffe, Kayes,

Marek, Mills, Odorizzi, Orth, Sacks, Brig. Gen. Sarnoff, R. Sarnoff, Saxon, Seidel, Teegarden, Tuft, Watts, Weaver, Werner, Williams

Gentlemen: An important message intended expressly for your eyes is now on its way to each one of you by special messenger.

William H. Weintraub & Company, Inc. *Advertising* *488 Madison Avenue, New York*

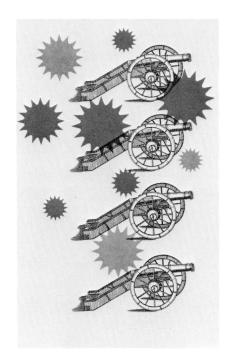

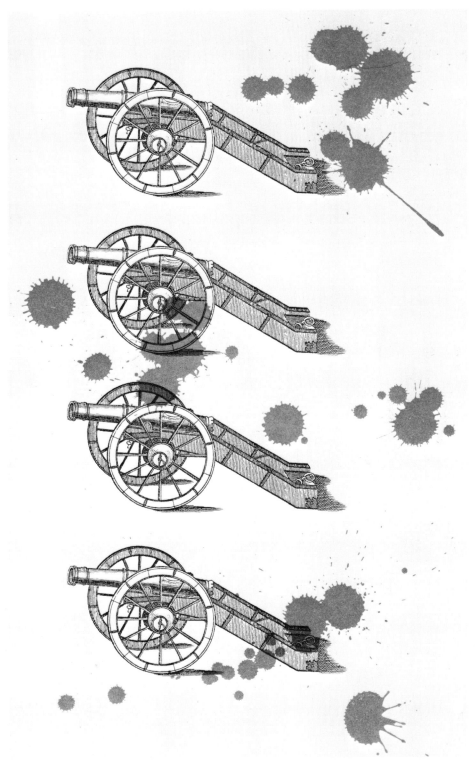

In this classic design, Paul Rand takes advantage of symbols that his targeted audience is familiar with. In this advertisement, directed to the executives and management personnel of RCA, the symbols of Morse code that spell out RCA are compared with an exclamation mark.

The two battle scenes from *A Young Patriot in the American Revolution* display Bradbury Thompson's ability to capture the essence of his messages in direct and powerful ways.

ONE NINE SEVEN SEVEN

Clarence Lee uses substitution to create clever Christmas cards. In the one for 1977, he divides the word *seven* to make a double-digit number. For 1981, he adds two letters in an unpredictable, but at once familiar, manner.

1 9 8 ONE

Two Turns
Twenty-Five!

25

And we're turning Channel 2 Night at Pops into a very special birthday celebration— exclusively for you.

Come join the WGBH family for an unforgettable night: glorious music by the Boston Pops conducted by Maestro John Williams; a special guest star; an audience and stage sprinkled with your favorite Channel 2 personalities; and birthday champagne at every table.

What we need to make the evening really special—is you! Won't you join us at a table in Symphony Hall on Friday, May 2 at 8pm as Two Turns Twenty-Five?

Yes! ○ I want to be in on the exclusive Two Turns Twenty-Five fun. Here's my check for $250 for a table.

Only tables on the floor are available. There are 5 seats to a table. $190 is tax-deductible. Tickets will be mailed after April 7, 1980. Reservations will be filled in the order of checks received, so hurry—there are only 180 tables!

Sorry! ○ I can't join the fun, but I'd like to contribute $_____ as a 25th birthday gift to Channel 2.

Name

Address

City   State   Zip

Telephone

Tom Sumida designed these fund-raising announcements to celebrate WGBH-TV's 25th anniversary: 2 turns 25. Note that the integrity of the 2 (for Channel 2) has been maintained.

Now we stand on the threshold of the next 25 years—a future in which program ideas are blossoming, technological advances are breaking, and costs are rising faster than ever before. It is to meet these exciting—and costly—challenges with renewed strength and confidence that we look to you to support a very special 25th birthday fundraising endeavor. We call it our *Two Turns Twenty-Five Birthday Fund*—and we look to it and to you to give us the extra push we need to launch us into the future.

Your *Two Turns Twenty-Five Birthday Fund* gift is vital to us in three important areas:

1 to firmly establish an endowment for WGBH

2 to provide unrestricted funds for new local programming initiatives

3 to provide working and planning capital for us to explore the wide range of telecommunications options opening to us now and in years to come.

All of the programs represented in these pictures are produced by WGBH and are made available to public television stations throughout the nation. This is an example of WGBH's 25 year contribution to the Public Broadcasting Service.

wment
...*Two Turns Twenty-* ...gift will help ...gthen our growing ...wment. Just two ...s ago, our endow- ...t stood at only ...00. Now, thanks to ...entrated efforts on ...art of our new

Planned Giving office, it's nearly $1 million. Please help us boost that to $2.5 million in 1980, in honor of our first 25 years.

2 Local Programming
Your *Two Turns Twenty-Five* gift will help bolster the vitally important un-restricted funds so neces-sary for the development of new local programming initiatives. Remember that programs such as *Julia Child & Company, Evening at Symphony, Crockett's Victory Garden* and *ZOOM* are among the many national PBS favor-ites which began as local programs on Channel 2. Your contribution will allow

us to put our money and efforts into new and crea-tive program ideas which will eventually fund them-selves and repay us with a flow of income we can plow back into trying out new ideas. Our goal is $250,000 in unrestricted funds for local programming.

3 Capital for the Future
Your *Two Turns Twenty-Five* gift will go towards planning our future in a very real way. The revolu-tion in telecommunica-tions technology is changing our world faster and faster. It brings with it a challenging array of threats and opportuni-ties: multiple distribution systems via satellite, cable and pay cable, videodiscs and cassettes, teletext (which offers viewers random access to

a wide range of text and graphic displays on home TV receivers), over-the-air subscription services, and more. The choices in-crease quickly, and affect the heart of our work in communications. We need capital—$250,000— to explore the opportuni-ties open to us—and to initiate our own—so that non-commercial broad-casting survives and thrives in the 1980s.

From the first newscast by Louis Lyons to "The First Churchills" on *Master-piece Theatre*...from how to cook with *The French Chef* to how to renovate your own home with *This Old House*...WGBH has brought 25 years of enter-taining, stimulating, and informative program-

ming of the highest quality to millions of viewers throughout our city, our state, our country, and, indeed, all over the world.

Please join us in this very special effort to com-memorate our past and to ensure our future.

This Dubonnet poster ad is an excellent example of comparative play with symbols. In French, *Dubo* means "something liquid," *Dubon* means "something good," and *Dubonnet* is a special wine. A. H. Cassandre emphasizes the message by repeating word and image in a witty sequence.

GOING TO SEE THE SOUTH AFRICAN 'WHITES ONLY' CRICKET TEAM?

(IT'S NOT CRICKET)

Bob Gill uses a verbal pun to give impact to his message in this poster.

The husband-and-wife design team of Millward and Millward, Inc. reinforces their union through this logo with its thick and thin, hard and soft letterforms.

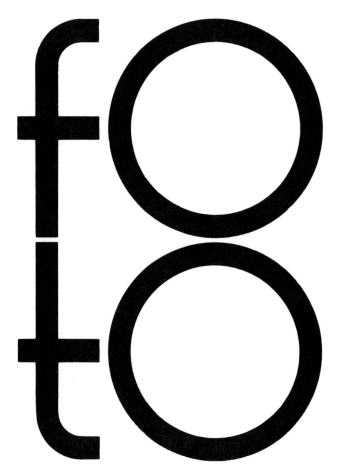

Ditto Ditto

The substitution of the ditto mark for the dot of the *i* in this logo for Ditto results in a comparison of sound / symbol and visual imagery.

George Tscherny plays on the similarity in appearance of the letters *f* and *t* to make one seem to reflect the other in this logo.

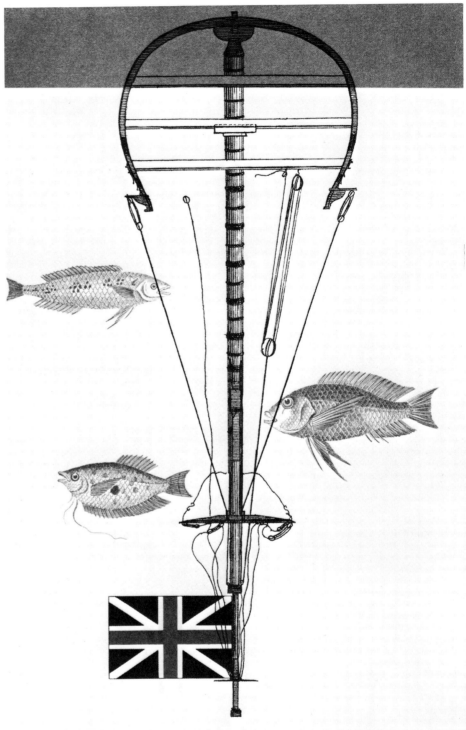

Bradbury Thompson often takes advantage of the sequential quality of books to create puns. On the divider pages in *A Young Patriot in the American Revolution*, the main symbol, the ship, is unaltered, while the secondary symbols—the birds and fish—are changed to create a strong impact.

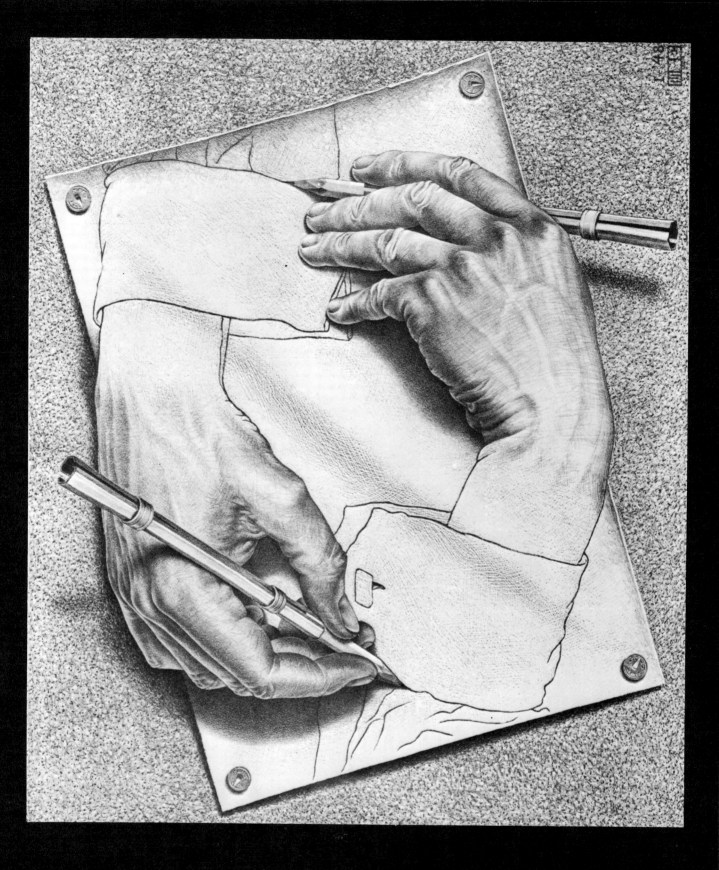

6
NO
PUN
INTENDED

The concept of visual pollution has become a cliché. But the problem that gave rise to the term persists. Visual communicators often have no alternative but to post messages in the midst of a profusion of other messages. Whether images are to be displayed in public places or in printed media, designers have the same responsibility: to attract attention, to persuade the viewer, and to motivate the person to take action. There are many ways to do this effectively. Puns are one, but there are also other ways to play with symbols and still create effective communication. Exploring the different types of image play that do not fall under the heading of puns is the purpose of this chapter. The following discussion of optical illusion, ambiguity, paradox, metaphor, metamorphosis, and cartoons will make the distinctions clear.

Optical Illusion

Perception is the key in optical illusions. What we see can't be, but is. Our senses seem to be deceiving us. How can one object be two different things at the same time? The Necker cube, a familiar example, has six possible readings, while the Brown University logo designed by Malcolm Grier is just as unique. Both images flop at will. Although we know they are only one image, the point of perspective shifts constantly. Beyond our will or control, the eye cannot choose one viewpoint and is forced to shift repeatedly from one to the other. The two-pronged trident is an even more confounding illusion. We expect to see three prongs, but find only two. What at first appears obvious becomes impossible. Our expectations have been tricked, and there ensues a timeless battle of right or wrong.

Illusions devised by cognitive psychologists are also worth noting, such as the bent ruler effect created by R. L. Gregory and E. H. Gombrich. The rulers appear to be bulging near their centers when a spoked wheel is superimposed on them. One element influences the other, and we are mentally challenged to accept the results. While such an illusion can suggest different possibilities or meanings, the integrity of the symbols being combined are optically altered and distorted in the process.

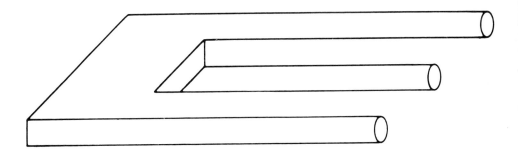

M. C. Esher's *Drawing Hands* is a classic statement on the art of illusion.

Developed by cognitive psychologist R. L. Gregory, the two-pronged trident is a simple line drawing that creates a particularly perplexing optical illusion.

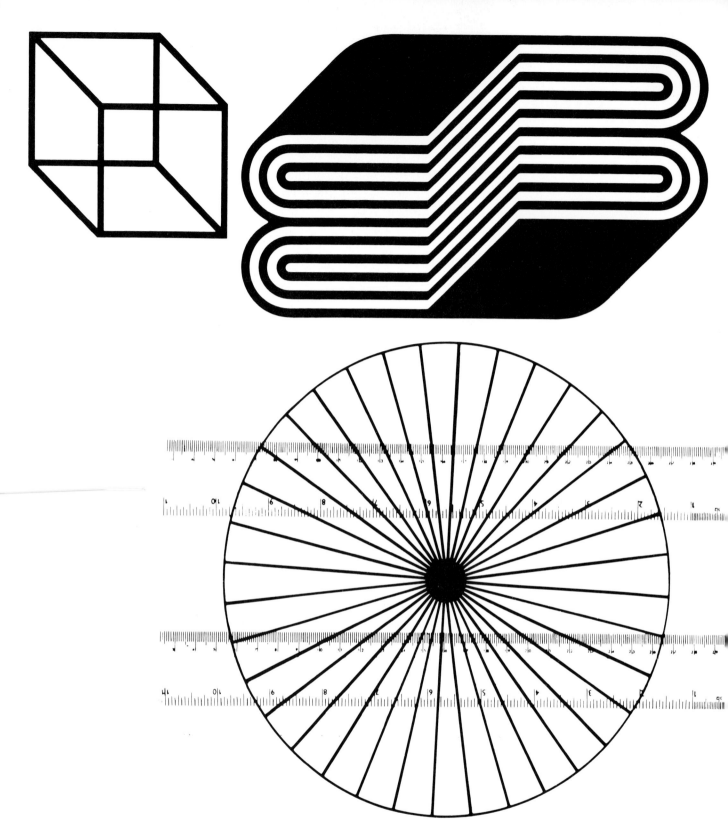

There are six possible ways to read the Necker cube, an optical illusion created to study cognitive perception. The mind accepts each of the possible solutions, but can never settle on one.

The Brown University press logo, an optical illusion created by Malcolm Grier, does not give the mind an opportunity to locate a fixed viewpoint.

A bent ruler is not possible, but that is how we perceive it when a spoked wheel is superimposed on it.

Ambiguity

One image can be viewed as two or more possible objects at the same time. They play on your point of reference. Two excellent examples of ambiguity are Winson's "Indian or Eskimo" figure, showing two different cultures and climates, and E. G. Boring's "Mother-in-Law," with its comparison of youth and age. Both combine opposite and conflicting realities in one drawing. One image works as two. However, as with illusions, we can only focus on one at a time.

There is a similarity of technique in figure/ground reversals. Edgar Rubin's classic illustration (shown on page 32) relies on the space between two faces to create a vase. What we see fluctuates, vying for visual superiority. The Eaton corporation logo also plays with positive and negative space, though only one image is formed. The positive forms incorporate the missing letters so that we can read the whole word.

This study in perceptual ambiguity, created by Winson, compares people of two widely differing cultures and climates.

The logo for Eaton Corporation is legible even though two letters are "missing."

E. G. Boring's ambiguous mother-in-law image, created to advance the study of cognitive perception, can be seen as both an old lady and a young woman.

Paradox

One image can contain two meanings, but in a paradox the meanings are contradictory and totally impossible. Milton Glaser designed a paradox in his poster for the School of Visual Arts, bringing together two disparate disciplines in one image. His treatment is similar to that used on Victorian vases or on other decorated sculptural pieces of art. Because of its implausibility, a paradox can be exciting and arresting.

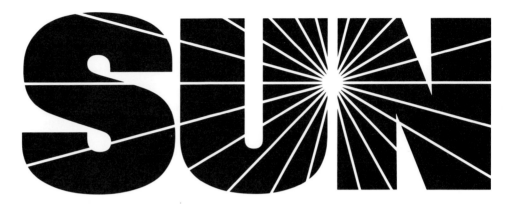

Milton Glaser creates a paradoxical situation by overlapping disparate symbols in this poster for the School of Visual Arts.

The Sun Company logo, designed by Anspach Grossman Portugal, expresses the essence of energy while at the same time reflecting the company's name.

A bargain too good
to last

Mobil

Metaphor

Translating a concept into an image or putting an image into another format that is analogous is a visual metaphor. Hence, the term *visual translation*. The images are chosen to illustrate the message, and there is no hint of a double meaning or more than one interpretation. Sometimes a metaphor may at first appear to be a literal pun, but after an analysis of the role of its symbols, it will become clear that the symbols simply function to visualize a very specific concept. The Best logo on page 42 is a clear example of a metaphor. The letters were manipulated to convey the concept of growth and expansion. The design firm of Chermayeff & Geismar Associates changed the height and thickness of each letter in the three-dimensional version of the logo. The shortest letter—the *B*—is also the fattest.

Although the Best logo was created by symbol manipulation, metaphors are usually created by combining symbols that at first appear incompatible. For instance, Danne & Blackburn illustrated the weakening of the dollar with a stone dollar crumbling. Commenting on the rising cost of transportation, Joseph Bottoni composed a dollar sign with arrows shot from different directions. Metaphors are deliberately created to stimulate the mind—Magritte, the master of the metaphor, described his work as painting ideas.

This poster by Danne & Blackburn Inc. captures the message with a monetary symbol made of crumbling stone.

Joseph Bottoni uses arrows to compose a dollar sign in this poster for the Cincinnati Tri-State Transportation Conference. The message is reinforced by the arrows moving in and out of the format.

1977
Cincinnati
Tri-State
Transportation
Conference

Transportation services can no longer continue to grow without both citizens and professionals coming to an agreement on what is to be done, how services can be coordinated, and how they are to be funded.

That is what the 1977 Cincinnati Tri-State Transportation Conference is all about.

How
Do We
Go
From
Here?

The conference will take place on Thursday, February 10 and Friday, February 11, 1977 at the Cincinnati Convention Center at Fifth and Elm Streets. It is sponsored by the Ohio-Kentucky-Indiana Regional Council of Governments (OKI) and co-sponsored by many organizations representing various transportation interests in the region.

Previous conferences held in June 1972 and October 1974, involved evaluation of the transportation needs of the Cincinnati Tri-State area and discussion of effective solutions.

In 1972, the emphasis was public ownership of the private transit system. The conference helped to organize support around that issue and lead to the passage of the 0.3% earnings tax transit levy in November 1972.

In 1974, the conference theme was, 'Where Do We Go From Here?' Proposals for improvements to serve the area's transportation needs were presented and discussed.

Since the 1974 conference it has become apparent that the region's ability to serve its transportation needs requires consensus on both current and future transportation plans and adequate financing to implement them.

Who Can Participate?

The conference is designed to bring state and federal officials together with local public officials, business leaders, agency representatives, and interested citizens to discuss united goals and programs for achieving transportation improvements in the Cincinnati Tri-State area.

What Will We Talk About?

Conference sessions and speakers will present plans and proposals currently under development. Capital and operating costs, and benefits of the proposed improvements will be described. The conference participants will then use plans, costs, and benefits to develop the theme, 'How Do We Go From Here? Transportation Systems Management Programs for Action will be presented in such subject areas as:
1. Passenger movement between regions
2. Passenger movements within regions
3. Goods movement between regions
4. Goods movement within regions
5. Transportation between adjacent communities sharing major travel arteries
6. Special programs such as elderly and handicapped services, bikeways, etc.

Specific Topics

1. Lightrail transit
2. Downtown people mover system
3. Ohio River port development
4. Highway development in the Colerain Avenue and Little Miami River Valley areas
5. Multi-use terminals and distribution systems for goods
6. Completion of the inter-state highway system
7. Improved transit services for the elderly and handicapped
8. Inter-city rail passenger services

Summary

The programs that emerge from the conference sessions will consider current federal and state transportation policies and will emphasize relationships between the needs for improved services and the availability of funds to provide them. Efficiencies will be addressed, new funding sources will be evaluated, and an on-going program to develop funding support will be defined.

'How Do We Go From Here?' is the theme: The political and business leaders and citizens of the region are both audience and participants; and current transportation issues are the subject which the 1977 Cincinnati Tri-State Transportation Conference is designed to address.

 Cincinnati Tri-State
Transportation Conference

The American Short Story

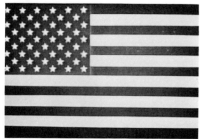

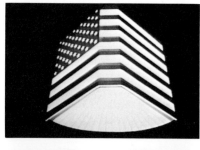

The problem here was to convey in the few seconds leading into a TV show the idea of American literature translated onto film. Animation, which allows the metamorphosis from one familiar visual metaphor to another, facilitates the rather easy delivery of a fairly complex idea.

Metamorphosis

Images can change, moving sequentially from one into another, in a metamorphosis. This technique plays on the likeness of symbols and relies on shape, size, contrast, or motion to alter them. For metamorphosis to be effective, the designer must constantly search for new associations and versatility with the spectrum of symbols. One example is the opening to "The American Short Story" produced by WGBH-TV in Boston with its flag-to-book-to-film sequence—a moving metaphor.

Cartoon

The story-telling process of the cartoon doesn't demand that images change in a related sequence, only that the sequence be used to create a story. Often animating inanimate objects, the cartoon is frequently used to convey conventional ideas in cute, but standard, treatments. Milton Glaser's series showing Mozart sneezing is a particularly apt example.

In this illustration, Milton Glaser creates a clever cartoon sequence of Mozart sneezing.

Many perceptual effects and playful images have the power to evoke strong responses and immediate sensations, and they are a designer's most important resources. While many ideas originating in other fields of study can be applied to graphic design, original research by graphic designers can generate information that may in turn have an effect on other fields. The possibilities are boundless. It's up to the designer to explore the uncharted galaxies of visual space, with puns as the stars.

Helvetica

By using a serif typeface, Jack Summerford deliberately creates ambiguity in his poster for the most widely used sans serif typeface.

DAVID'S lemonade

DAVID'S lemonade

DAVID'S lemonade

In this portfolio piece for Sanders Printing, Fulton & Partners play on the concept of corporate identities. For his lemonade sales, David was given a corporate identity with a special typeface in regular, medium, and bold.

ARCHITECTURAL & ENGINEERING
NEWS

Building Research

Chermayeff & Geismar Associates designed these *Architectural & Engineering News* jackets with ambiguous images suggesting buildings.

In 1972 Best Inc. commissioned Site to develop a series of special showrooms—each a unique work of art related to its environment—in various locations throughout the U.S. These projects are also a commentary on the "integration" of art and architecture, becoming simultaneously both a monument and a building. The ones shown here are located in Richmond, Virginia (above), and Houston, Texas.

Richard Haas enjoys painting metaphoric wall murals, whether on Prince Street, where most of the buildings do have windows or in Times Square, where such a building could exist.

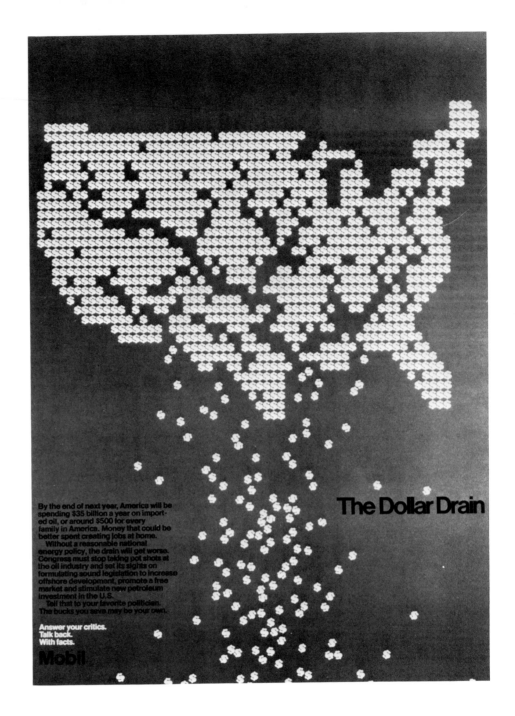

Within the image:
The Dollar Drain

By the end of next year, America will be spending $35 billion a year on imported oil, or around $500 for every family in America. Money that could be better spent creating jobs at home.

Without a reasonable national energy policy, the drain will get worse. Congress must stop taking pot shots at the oil industry and set its sights on formulating sound legislation to increase offshore development, promote a free market and stimulate new petroleum investment in the U.S.

Tell that to your favorite politician. The bucks you save may be your own.

Answer your critics.
Talk back.
With facts.

Mobil

Greg Brown has painted fantasy murals on walls (top) and mirrors (below) that tease one's sense of reality. His metaphoric scenes shake the imagination as they play with our hidden desires.

Danne & Blackburn Inc. combine dollar signs to suggest both the United States and depletion of money on imported oil.

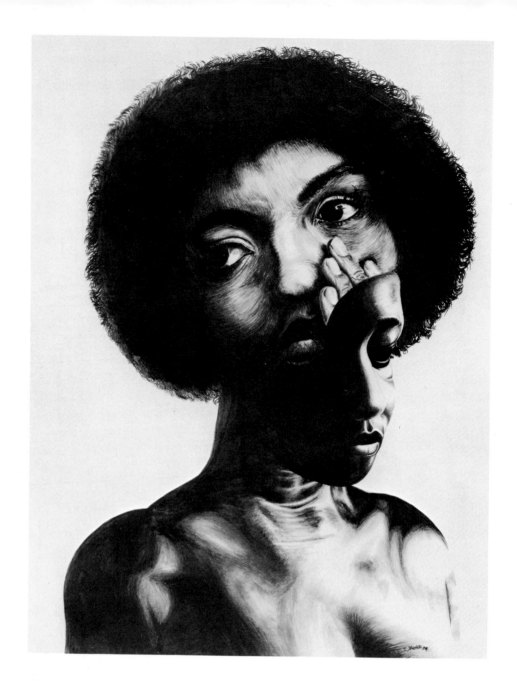

Eli Kince creates ambiguity in this illustration of realities overlapping in a surrealistic manner.

Charles Lilly uses sequence and transition to visualize his concept of Malcolm X's life in this poster that relies on metaphor.

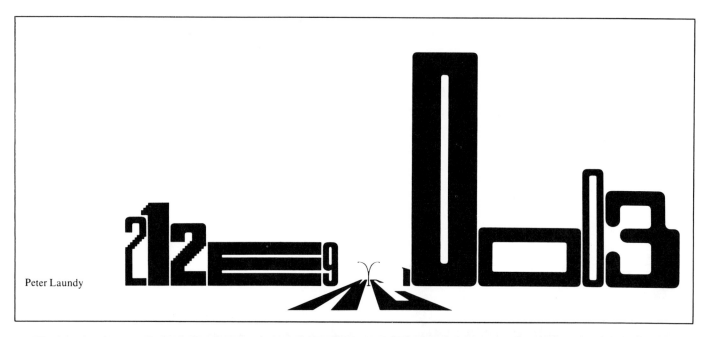

Peter Laundy

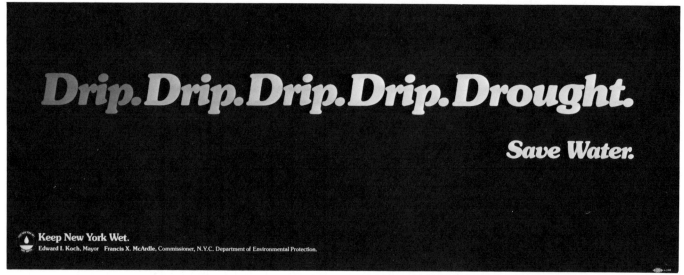

Drip. Drip. Drip. Drip. Drought.

Save Water.

Keep New York Wet.
Edward I. Koch, Mayor   Francis X. McArdle, Commissioner, N.Y.C. Department of Environmental Protection.

Peter Laundy visually translates his address to suggest buildings and streets.

The Department of Environmental Protection in New York City played on the repetitious sound of a leaky faucet to create this effective message about a water shortage.

In a promotional booklet for Mead Paper Co., Reynold Ruffins visually translates the phrases, ''between the devil and the deep blue sea'' and ''stool pigeon,'' to create metaphors.

157

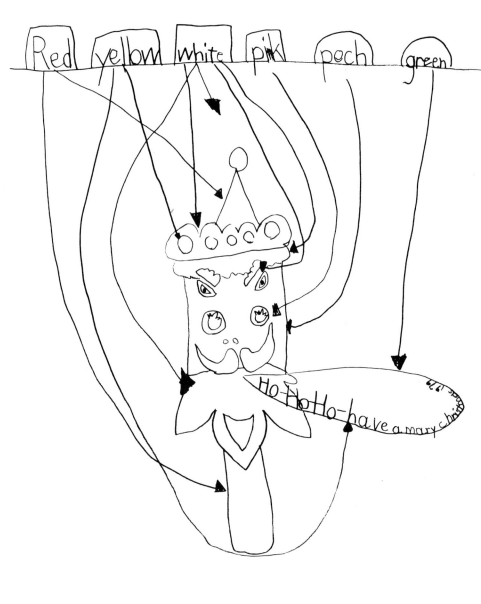

Red yellow white pink pech green

Ho-Ho-Ho-have a mary christmas

Cliff Dawson, using ambiguity, created a bird house in the form of a face, with a tongue that doubles as a perch.

Joseph Bottoni created a one-frame cartoon by substituting words for colors in this Christmas card drawn by his son.

This cartoon fantasy animates a record cover called ''Toot Suite'' for CBS Records.

Chermayeff & Geismar Associates
created a symbol for the White House
Conference on Children in 1970 and
then manipulated it in a variety of situations.

Emergence of Identity

Expressions of Identity

Crisis in Values

Future of Learning

Creativity and the Learning Process

The Right to Read

Myths of Education

Educational Hardware

Keeping Children Healthy

Making Children Healthy

Handicapped

Injured

Changing Families

Children and Parents

Family Planning Family Economics

Child Care

Children Without Prejudice

Environment

Child Development and Mass Media

Leisure Time

Rights of Children

Children in Trouble

The Child Advocate

Communicating the Law

Child Service Institutions

CREDITS

59 Art director/designer: Dick Lemmon; writer: Martin Dawson; photographer: Tony Petrucelli; agency: Zechman and Associates, Chicago. Reprinted by permission of the American Library Association.

60 Designer: Ian James Wright; client: ASH (Action against Smoking & Health), 1974.

61 Designed by Bradbury Thompson. Reprinted with permission from Westvaco Corporation.

62 Left: Art director: Ron Becker; writer: Anita Baron; creative director: Peter Hirsch; agency: DKG, New York; client; Talon Zippers, 1975. Courtesy Talon, Inc.

62 Right: Art director: Ron Becker; writer: Anita Baron; creative director: Peter Hirsch; photographer: 20th Century Fox—Mel Brooks; illustrator: Arton Associates; agency: DKG, New York; client: Talon Zippers, 1975. Courtesy Talon, Inc.

63 Designed by Joseph Bottoni.

64 Left: Art: C. Piccirillo; copy: T. Bell; Agency: Doyle Dane Bernbach, 1981. Courtesy Chivas Regal Scotch Whiskey.

64 Right: Art: Jim Scalfone; copy: Diane Rothschild; agency: Doyle Dane Bernbach, 1977. Courtesy Chivas Regal Scotch Whiskey.

65 Art director: Tom Donovan; copywriter: Dick Thomas: agency; Bozell & Jacobs, Inc., Minneapolis. Courtesy Northwestern Bell Telephone Company.

66 Armin Hofmann, *Baur*, 1979. On extended loan to The Museum of Modern Art, New York, from the artist.

67 Designer: Inge Druckrey; client: Yale Symphony Orchestra.

68 Designed by Bradbury Thompson. Reprinted with permission from Westvaco Corporation.

70 Left: Courtesy Alcoa.

70 Right: Designed by John Massey, Center for Advance Research in Design, for the American Library Association. Reprinted by permission of the American Library Association.

71 Courtesy L'eggs Products, Inc.

72 Design: Chris Pullman, John Kayne, Gay Korbet; client: WGBH-Boston.

73 Designer: Lance Wyman; assistant designer: Stephen Schlott; client: Minnesota Zoo, Apple Valley, Minnesota.

74 Agency: Danne & Blackburn Inc.

75 Left: Designed by Rudolph De Harak.

75 Right: Designed by Orietta Arroyo, student in class taught by Lance Wyman, Parsons School of Design, New York.

76 Designed by Rudolph De Harak.

77 Designed by Peter Millward.

78 Left: RABBIT HEAD Design is a trademark of and used with permission of Playboy Enterprises, Inc.

78 Right: Agency: Danne & Blackburn Inc.

79 Designed by Herb Lubalin, Lubalin, Peckolick Assoc. Inc.

80-81 Designed by Alan Fletcher, Pentagram Graphic Design Consultants.

82 Designed by Eli Kince.

83 Designed by Bradbury Thompson. Reprinted with permission from Westvaco Corporation.

84 © Time Inc.

85 Courtesy Volkswagen of America.

86 Gordon Salchow/Graphic Designer.

87 Art director: Barbara Schubeck; writer: Bob Nadler; creative directors: Sam Scali/Ed McCabe; photographer: Phil Marco; agency: Scali McCabe Sloves, New York; client: U.S. Pioneer Electronics.

88 Designed by Dan Reisinger, 1969, Israel.

89 Designed by Eli Kince.

90 Designed by Rand Schuster.

91 Designed by Paul Rand. Courtesy The New York Art Directors Club and the artist.

92 Left: Designed by Bob Gill.

92 Right: Art director/designer: Louis Dorfsman, CBS.

93 Top: Designed by Tony Palladino.

93 Bottom: Art director: Lars Anderson; copywriter: Rodney Underwood; photographer: Jerry Friedman; agency: Scali McCabe Sloves.

94 Artist: Jerry Pinkney.

95 Designed by Bradbury Thompson. Reprinted with permission from Westvaco Corporation.

96 Top: Pentagram Graphic Design Consultants.

96 Bottom: Chermayeff & Geismar Associates.

97 Left: Giuseppe Arcimboldo, *Portrait of Rudolf II as Vertumnus*, c. 1590. Nationalmuseum, Stockholm. Courtesy Skoklosters Slott.

97 Right: Giuseppe Arcimboldo, *The Librarian*, 1565. Nationalmuseum, Stockholm. Courtesy Skoklosters Slott.

98 Designed by Russell Leong, Russell Leong Design Group.

99 Designed by Paul Rand. Courtesy the American Institute of Graphic Arts. Quote in caption from Champion Papers, *The Printing Salesman Herald*, Book 35.

100 Art director: Advertising Designers, Inc./Tom Ohmer; designer: Carl Seltzer; typography: Advertising Designers Type Shop; client: Advertising Designers, Inc.

101 Art director: Lars Hall (Arbmans Advertising Agency); photographer: Bertil Strandell; client: Ateljé von Sterneck 1971 (now Studio Tranan Ab, Stockholm).

102 Art director: Phil Silvestri; copywriter: Rita Senders; creative director: Ron Travisano; agency: Della Femina, Travisano & Partners, Inc.; advertiser/client: WABC-TV/Jon Olken.

103 Created for Levi's® Movin'On™ Jeans by Terry Lamb. © Levi Strauss & Co., 1981.

104 Artist: Greg Brown; client: University National Bank, Palo Alto, CA; photographer: Carl J. Schmitt.

105 Designed by Colin Forbes, Pentagram Graphic Design Consultants.

106 Designed by Valerie Pettis.

107 Designed by Paul Rand. Courtesy National Park Service and the artist.

108 Designed by Henry Wolf for *Esquire*, April 1955. Copyright © 1955 by Esquire Publishing Inc.

109 Designed by Sheila Levrant de Bretteville.

110 Armin Hofmann, *Wilhelm Tell*, 1963. Collection, The Museum of Modern Art, New York. Gift of the artist.

111 Chermayeff & Geismar Associates.

112 Designed by Mervyn Kurlansky, Pentagram Graphic Design Consultants.

113 Designer: George Tscherny; client: Overseas National Airways (ONA), 1968.

114 Artist: Who Ever; art direction: John Berg. Courtesy CBS Records.

115 Designer: Lance Wyman; assistant designer: Stephen Schlott; client: Minnesota Zoo, Apple Valley, Minnesota.

116 Illustrator/art director: Seymour Chwast; designer: Richard Mantel; design firm: Push Pin Studios, Inc., March/April 1980.

118 Lubalin, Peckolick Assoc. Inc.

119 Designed by Paul Rand.

120 Designed by Bob Gill.

121 Designed by Bradbury Thompson. Reprinted with permission from Westvaco Corporation.

122 Designed by Bradbury Thompson. Reprinted with permission from Westvaco Corporation.

123 Designer: Paul Rand, 1954; client: William H. Weintraub & Co. Advertising Agency.

124 Designed by Clarence Lee.

126-127 Designer: Tom Sumida; design manager: Chris Pullman, WGBH-Boston.

128-129 A. M. Cassandre, *Dubo Dubon Dubonnet*, 1932. Collection, The Museum of Modern Art, New York. Gift of Bernard Davis.

130 Designed by Bob Gill.

131 Designed by Peter Millward and Ruth Millward.

132 Designed by Bradbury Thompson. Reprinted with permission from Westvaco Corporation.

133 Left: Courtesy ATF-Davidson Company, Division of White Consolidated Industries, Inc.

133 Right: Designer: George Tscherny, 1968; client: foto-graphics.

134 M. C. Escher, *Drawing Hands*. © BEELDRECHT, Amsterdam/VAGA, New York. Collection Haags Gemeentemuseum, The Hague, 1981.

135 R. L. Gregory, *The Intelligent Eye*, McGraw-Hill Book Company.

136 Top right and bottom: R. L. Gregory, *The Intelligent Eye*, McGraw-Hill Book Company.

136 Top left: Designed by Malcolm Grear in 1963 for Brown University Press.

137 Top right and left: R. L. Gregory, *The Intelligent Eye*, McGraw-Hill Book Company.

137 Bottom left: Courtesy Eaton Corporation, Cleveland, OH.

138 Design and illustration by Milton Glaser.

139 Courtesy Sun Company, Inc.

140 Danne & Blackburn Inc.

141 Designed by Joseph Bottoni.

142 Design Manager: Chris Pullman, WGBH-Boston.

143 Design and illustration by Milton Glaser.

144 Designer: Jack Summerford; design firm: Summerford Design, Inc.; client: Typographics.

145 *David's Lemonade*, Corporate Identity Manual, Folio 15, Sanders Printing Corporation, New York; concept/design: Fulton + Partners Inc., New York; photographer: Laurence Robins © 1976.

146 Chermayeff & Geismar Associates.

147 Chermayeff & Geismar Associates.

148 The Best Products Co., Inc., showroom, Richmond, VA. Project designers: SITE PROJECTS, New York. Courtesy Best Products Co., Inc.

149 The Best Products Co., Inc., showroom, Houston, TX 1975. Project designers: SITE PROJECTS, New York; architects: Maples-Jones Associates, Fort Worth, TX. Courtesy Best Products Co., Inc., Richmond, VA.

150 Richard Haas, *112 Prince St. Façade*, New York, 1974–1975. Commissioned by City Walls, Inc. Photo Courtesy Public Art Fund.

151 Richard Haas, *The Times Tower*, New York, 1979. Commissioned by 42nd Street Redevelopment Corporation. Photograph by Jacob Bruckhardt.

152 Top: © Greg Brown Muralist (Concord, CA). Photo by Dewey Dellinger.

153 Bottom: © Greg Brown, Muralist (San Francisco, CA).

153 Danne & Blackburn Inc.

154 Designed by Eli Kince.

155 Artist: Charles Lilly; client: Encore Communications.

156 Designer/artist: Reynold Ruffins; client: Mead Paper, Fine Paper Division.

157 Top: Designed by Peter Laundy.

157 Bottom: Art director: Annette G. Ahlmann; artist: Steve Zwillinger; printer: Lubert Press, Inc.; agency: Leonard G. Styche and Associates, Inc.; date: 1981. Reprinted by permission of New York City Department of Environmental Protection.

158 Left top and bottom: Designer: Clifford Dawson; photo: Armand Wright.

158 Right: Designed by Joseph Bottoni.

159 Artist: Who Ever; art direction: John Berg. Courtesy CBS Records.

160-161 Chermayeff & Geismar Associates.

SELECTED BIBLIOGRAPHY

Albers, Joseph. *Interaction of Color.* New Haven, Conn.: Yale University Press, 1975.

Barr, Alfred. *Cubism and Abstract Art.* New York: Museum of Modern Art, 1936.

Berger, John. *Ways of Seeing.* New York: Pelican Books, Inc., 1972.

Carter, Thomas F. *The Invention of Printing in China and Its Spread Westward.* New York: Roland Press, 1955.

Chao, Yuen-Ren. *Language and Symbolic Systems.* New York: Cambridge University Press, 1968.

Cheat, Bernard. *Art of Drawing.* New York: Holt, Rinehart & Winston, Inc., 1970.

Craig, James. *Designing with Type: A Basic Course in Typography.* Rev. ed. New York: Watson-Guptill Publications, 1980.

_____. *Phototypesetting: A Design Manual.* New York: Watson-Guptill Publications, 1978.

_____. *Production for the Graphic Designer.* New York: Watson-Guptill Publications, 1974.

Dreyfuss, Henry. *Symbol Source Book.* New York: McGraw-Hill Book Co., 1972.

Fabre, Maurice. *A History of Communication.* New York: Hawthorn Books, 1963.

Gerstner, Karl. *Compendium for Literates.* Cambridge, Mass.: MIT Press, 1974.

Gombrich, Ernest. *Art and Illusion.* Princeton, N.J.: Princeton University Press, 1961.

_____. *Symbolic Images.* New York: Praeger Pubs., 1972.

Gregory, R. L. *Eye and Brain.* New York: McGraw-Hill Book Co., 1973.

Herbert, Robert L. *Modern Artist on Art.* Englewood Cliffs, N.J.: Prentice-Hall, Inc., 1964.

Hofmann, Armin. *Graphic Design Manual.* New York: Van Nostrand Reinhold Co., 1965.

Klee, Paul. *Diaries 1898-1918.* Berkeley, Calif.: University of California Press, 1964.

_____. *The Thinking Eye.* London: Lund Humphries, 1961.

Koestler, Arthor. *The Act of Creation.* New York: Macmillan Publishing Co., Inc., 1953.

Leger, Fernard. *Functions of Paintings.* New York: Viking Press, Inc., 1973.

Le Corbusier. *Towards a New Architecture.* New York: Praeger Pubs., 1970.

Lissitzky, El. *Catalogue.* Cologne: Galerie Gmurzynska, 1974.

Maholy-Nagy, Laszlo. *Visions in Motion.* Chicago: Paul Theobold & Co., 1947.

Malevitch, Kasimir. *Essays on Art.* New York: George Wittenborn Inc., 1975.

A Manual of Style. 12th ed. Chicago: University of Chicago Press, 1969.

Pentagram. *Living by Design.* Rev. ed. New York: Whitney Library of Design, 1979.

Pocket Pal: A Graphic Arts Production Handbook. International Paper Company, 1976.

Rand, Paul. *Thoughts on Design.* New York: Van Nostrand Reinhold Co., 1971.

Ricardson, Tony, ed. *Concepts of Modern Art.* New York: Harper & Row Pubs. Inc., 1974.

Ruder, Emil. *Typography.* New York: Hastings House Pubs. Inc., 1967.

Spencer, Herbert. *Pioneers of Modern Typography.* London: Lund Humphreys, 1969.

_____. *The Visible Word.* New York: Reinhold Pubs., 1967.

Steinberg, S. H. *500 Years of Printing.* New York: Penguin Books, Inc., 1974.

Stephenson, William. *The Play Theory of Mass Communication.* Chicago: University of Chicago Press, 1967.

Strunk, William. *Elements of Style.* New York: Macmillan Publishing Co., Inc., 1935.

Wentinck, Charles. *Modern and Primitive Art.* New York: Phaidon, 1974.

Wingler, Hans. *The Bauhaus.* Cambridge, Mass.: MIT Press, 1969.

Wolfflin, Heinrich. *Principles of Art History.* New York: Dover Pubns, Inc., 1915.

INDEX

Italics indicate illustrations